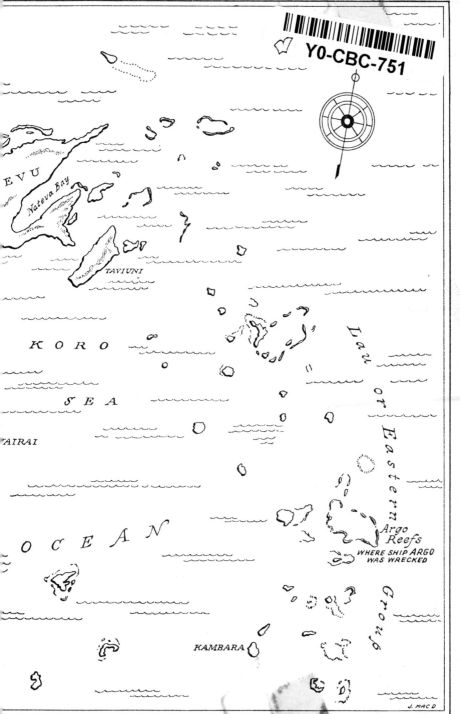

Y0-CBC-751

. 3ى

EVU

Nateva Bay

TAVIUNI

KORO

SEA

AIRAI

OCEAN

Lau or Eastern Group

Argo
Reefs
WHERE SHIP ARGO
WAS WRECKED

KAMBARA

J. MAC D

FIJI: *Islands of the Dawn*

919.61
W   Wibberley
                Fiji: Islands of the
          dawn

Ce⁵ ✓

Sierra Madre Public Library
Sierra Madre, California

OTHER BOOKS BY LEONARD WIBBERLEY

The Mouse on the Moon
The Mouse That Roared
Stranger at Killknock
The Hands of Cormack Joyce
Take Me to Your President
Beware of the Mouse
Coming of the Green
No Garlic in the Soup!
The Quest of Excalibur
The Land That Isn't There
Yesterday's Land
Ventures Into the Deep
The Time of the Lamb
Ballad of the Pilgrim Cat
Ah, Julian!
Feast of Freedom

919.61
W

FIJI:

Islands of the Dawn

By LEONARD WIBBERLEY

IVES WASHBURN, INC.

New York

SIERRA MADRE
PUBLIC LIBRARY
SIERRA MADRE
CALIFORNIA

FIJI: ISLANDS OF THE DAWN

COPYRIGHT © 1964 BY LEONARD WIBBERLEY

All rights reserved, including the right to reproduce
this book, or parts thereof, in any form, except for
the inclusion of brief quotations in a review.

LIBRARY OF CONGRESS CATALOG CARD NUMBER: 64-22144

MANUFACTURED IN THE UNITED STATES OF AMERICA

VAN REES PRESS • NEW YORK

Author's Note

I HAVE had a great deal of assistance from many people in writing this book and would like publicly to acknowledge this and thank them for their help.

No one can write about the Fiji Islands without constant reference to the works of Mr. R. A. Derrick. He is the true Boswell of Fiji—accurate, lively and exhaustive in his information and his two excellent books: *A History of Fiji* and *The Fiji Islands* are models of what a good history and a good geography of an area should be. As with Gibbon, Mr. Derrick's footnotes are even more interesting than his text. I have drawn heavily on his work and acknowledge with gratitude my debt to him.

Two Fiji residents were especially helpful to me—Captain Stanley B. Brown of the motor-sailer *Maroro*, and Mr. Rob Wright, Public Relations Officer in the Fiji government and one of the finest photographers in the South Pacific. His photographs have been widely used in internationally known publications, have been and are used in the design of postage stamps in Fiji, have won many awards for him, not least among them the Order of the British Empire from Queen Elizabeth II. Both these gentlemen supplied me with an immensity of information about the Fijis, always had time for me and loaned me books from their private libraries to help with my work. Certainly I could not have written this book without their help. Finally I must thank Mr. Don Lane of the Fiji Tourist Bureau for giving me the details of many Fiji legends. He has a huge collection of them, and was always able to find me accommodation whenever I turned up in the islands.

I have, of course, to go back to Fiji, for the islands are full of fascination for me. There are hundreds of them, each with its own story: one island on which there are strange stones with characters carved in a manner to suggest the work of the Chinese; another which is said to be tunneled completely through by the ocean. I would like to dive under it. At yet another there are sacred prawns, scarlet in color, which rise to the surface of a lake when the Fijians call them, and on still another there is a magnificent underground cavern, its entrance sealed off by the ocean, which is filled with blue light coming from below the water. Plainly, I must go back soon.

LEONARD WIBBERLEY

HERMOSA BEACH,
CALIFORNIA, 1964

FIJI: *Islands of the Dawn*

Chapter One

IF you will take a globe of the earth and put it before you so that the 170th meridian is about in the center, you will find the world turned to water. The whole hemisphere is an expanse of ocean framed with hesitant coasts of land—California and the western coast of America on your right and China and a furtive fringe of Australia on the left.

Between these lie the North and South Pacific oceans, the greatest uninterrupted expanse of water to be found on earth. Here the winds blow uninterrupted and undiverted by any great bulwarks of land in a pattern which has been established through billions of years. Here the tremendous ocean currents have their freest movement, swirling in two gigantic circles—one north and one south of the equator. The northern circle moves clockwise, the southern circle, anticlockwise. They almost meet, these two slow whirlpools, thousands of miles in size, at the equator and would carry a raft from Mexico to China without any other propulsion. Between them, however, is a countercurrent, flowing strongly east where they flow west, as if in the middle of a huge river, there was another stream which flowed in the opposite direction to the main body.

These magnificent ocean currents, which by their size make mere trickles of the largest rivers of land, form the communication network of the Pacific. Without them it is doubtful whether man or any mammals would have reached so early its hundreds of thousands of islands. These islands would have been, until the perfection of sail, barren spots known only perhaps to birds, and with vegetation restricted to such plants as could be seeded from bird droppings.

This vast ocean world divides orient from occident, and provides so great a barrier between East and West that western man first traversed it only five centuries ago and first managed to explore it thoroughly only two hundred years ago. The great waters defied him up to that time. Such an infinity of horizon lies there in the North and South Pacific that even today a traveler by jet plane feels after a while that he is caught motionless in a great blue bowl in which time and distance have dissolved.

Scattered over the ocean hemisphere, however, and especially in the western half, are thousands of islands. Some are no more than a crescent of sand behind a reef of coral on which the most graceful of all the world's trees grows —the coconut palm, a gift of the currents for it was brought by them from the Asiatic mainland. Its slender trunk soars upward to angle into the wind. It is the only tree which, rooted in the ground, appears to be leaping into the air.

You may tell the direction of the prevailing winds from the slope of the coconut palms whose topmost growth points unerringly into the wind's eye. On these smaller islands and islets there are sometimes other trees—the pandanus which is the tree of life in the Pacific and the tamarind and casuarina, again all gifts of the ocean current. But where there is an island of any size with a mountain range to cool the ocean-saturated air and produce rain, there is an exuberance of vegetable life so prolific that a score of different kinds of growth can readily be found in an acre. There are wild yams and cassava and tree ferns twenty feet and more in height— plants with leaves bigger than ears of elephants and grasses with blades like swords. Ferns of all kinds cling to every dripping, moss-hung cliff and every tree at which the sun can strike is festooned with vines, life living upon life so that it

2

is difficult, without looking carefully, to establish the nature of the tree itself.

Many of the smaller islands are still uninhabited, and you may, stepping ashore on a crescent of gleaming sand, find only the squitter of ghost crabs for tracks and not a human footprint or sign of humanity to be seen anywhere. There is a sad lost silence about such places which is broken only by the patter of the wind in the coconut fronds, the cry of terns and gulls fishing over the reef and the never-ending lapping of tiny wavelets on the beach. It takes considerable nerve to speak aloud and if you do the effect is shocking, as if you had shouted in a cathedral. The little white crabs on the beach are startled into immobility by the sound of your voice.

This was the condition of these islands when man first came to them. He came, as far as we know, from Asia and his land corridor to the sea was the Indonesian peninsula. He came by canoe or perhaps by raft. He could perhaps manage his craft to a limited extent with paddles or sails of matting, woven out of the leaves of the Tree of Life the pandanus. But paddles and sails were mere auxiliaries. His great engine was the ocean current that as soon as he left land—whether it was the Malay Peninsula or the great islands of Borneo, Sumatra or Java that he had already reached—swept him eastward. The current he used was undoubtedly that midstream equatorial current which runs steadily to the east while on both sides of it, north and south, the majestic countercurrents flow to the west. By clinging then to the equator he could travel east. By going to the north or the south he could travel west back whence he came. Probably over the generations he discovered this. But men do not commonly leave home in large numbers to return again. Once the land-dwelling Asian migrants had taken to their rafts and canoes and ventured into the ocean world of the Pacific, they stayed there. We can only guess why they made

3

the voyage at all, and the guess is that they were driven out of their homeland by better organized and aggressive invaders.

The first to come to the Pacific Islands, as far as we know, were small-boned, dark-skinned, fuzzy-haired people whom we call Papuans. They certainly traveled as far as New Guinea which is now their homeland and from there may have spread out to other islands and may even have reached the Fiji Islands—the Islands of the Dawn which lie a little west of the 180th meridian. Here, if the Papuans reached them, they stopped, for the Fijis are the last big islands of a petering chain which strikes into the Pacific south-southeast from Malaya. Beyond, to the east, lay open water and though there might be islands there, too, the evidence was that they would be smaller and smaller until eventually there would be none. Fiji, if they reached it, was their limit.

After the Papuans—no one knows how many generations or how many centuries later—came another wave of migrants. They were also dark skinned and fuzzy haired, but they were bigger boned and better skilled. They were farmers and basket weavers and pottery makers and carpenters and above all they were warriors. Their weapons were spears and slings, bows and arrows and throwing clubs. They were Stone Age people which means that they were also Bone and Wood Age people, these being the three raw materials out of which they made weapons and tools.

Their canoes were bigger than those of the Papuans and they may have been double hulled—two canoes joined by a platform on which a house was erected. They were propelled by mat sails and by paddles and of course the ocean currents.

These new invaders brought their gods with them, chief among them Ndengei, who has existed for all time in the form of a tremendous serpent but who concerns himself very little with human affairs. Other gods were the spirits of dead

4

chiefs because these people, who became known as Fijians, seem always to have had an unshakable belief in life after death. They had no altars or idols though they regarded certain trees and stones as sacred. Their favorite sport was war, and they warred both for the fun of killing and for the feast that followed since they ate the dead of battle.

Captives were also eaten, including women and children who might be brought back from a raid strung on poles like so many pigs.

The Fijians were part of the Melanesian or dark-skinned migration and Fiji marks the limit of their penetration into the Pacific. Some, it seems, did not reach the Pacific Islands at all. Their rafts or canoes were caught, perhaps west of Sumatra, in another current which swirled them across another ocean until they reached a place now called Tanganyika in Africa. There are significant similarities between the language of the Fijians and that of the people of Tanganyika, and there are customs and legends common to the two of them.

After the Fijian came light-skinned people with Mongolian rather than Negroid characteristics. Their skin was golden brown, their hair dark and straight, their eyes almond shaped, their chins small and their cheek bones high. They probably followed the same ancient route from Indonesia and finding now the whole island chain to the Fijis occupied, the greater part of them continued east to the Tuamotu and Society Islands and on to remote Easter Island, to the Marquesas and to Hawaii.

These, the Polynesians, were the greatest of the navigators. They became an ocean people, skilled in the currents and the winds. They were the Vikings of the Pacific and their far-questing canoes discovered New Zealand which they colonized and named Ao-tea-roa (the Long White Cloud) after viewing its snow-capped mountains on the southern horizon. One canoe went so far to the east as to discover the coast of Chile. But the voyagers found it inhospitable and returned and the great English navigator Cook was astounded when he heard the tale in Tahiti.

Some of these voyages of the Polynesians were accidental, the result of a canoe traveling from island to island being blown off its course by a gale. But many were deliberately planned explorations and by the time Alaric had taken Rome and Clovis had established himself as first King of the Franks, the greater part of the islands of the Pacific were occupied by the peoples whose descendants live on them today.

Among all these islanders the big, dark-skinned Fijians were spoken of with awe as a people devoted to continual warfare who delighted in feasting on human flesh. When the first Europeans reached the Pacific Islands and learned enough of the language to converse with the islanders, that was what they heard regarding the Fijians.

They called the Fiji group the Cannibal Islands and for centuries they avoided them. They were a place both beautiful and fearful at the same time—Paradise and the Inferno terribly merged into one.

Chapter Two

THE South Sea Islanders, Melanesian or Polynesian, had the Pacific on their doorstep when they started their ancient migration from the Asiatic mainland to their new homes. Europeans, not migrating but looking for riches, had to cross one ocean and then the Central American isthmus before even reaching the Pacific. They were centuries in doing this.

Originally some of the Europeans had been excellent sailors and they had built ships, such as the long ships of the Vikings, whose beauty has hardly been surpassed. The Viking ships were not only beautiful but seaworthy and from Scandinavia penetrated into the Black Sea and over to the American coast. Rather like the great Fijian and Polynesian canoes, they were ships for warriors and raiders and were not intended to carry cargo or engage in trade.

But when the people of Europe turned from raiding to trading, their skill as shipbuilders declined. Graceful, fast ships, designed to carry a hundred men, were replaced by sailing warehouses, with hulls like barrels, huge superstructures, and a tangle of rigging to support the masts and yards on which were stretched the sails that drove these lumbering craft through the water. They could move only with a fair wind and often had to be rowed when the wind would not serve. They trafficked chiefly in the Mediterranean and dared not venture past the Gate of Hercules into the rollers of the Atlantic for they would certainly founder. They held

7

back the sea exploration of the Europeans for perhaps a thousand years.

It was not until the end of the fifteenth century that Columbus made his Atlantic crossing, and the Pacific was still undreamed of. In making the crossing he used, like the early immigrants to the Pacific in their rafts, a current—the north equatorial current which swept him down to the West Indies. Had he headed north from there, he could have caught the Gulf Stream back to Europe.

It was indeed the Gulf Stream that gave Columbus one of his strongest clues to the existence of land on the other side of the Atlantic. A Portuguese pilot, Martin Vincente, blown in a westerly gale 1,200 miles into the ocean, found a piece of strange wood which had been carved floating in the water. The carving on the wood had not been done with iron tools. It had been brought from the West Indies by the Gulf Stream. Columbus' brother-in-law, Pedro Correa, found at Porto Santo in the Madeira Islands big canes capable of holding four quarts of wine between each joint—sections then of bamboo washed across the Atlantic by the Gulf Stream. But for the currents, the Pacific islanders might not have reached what was to become their homeland for many generations and the Europeans might not have discovered the American continent for a century or more.

After Columbus came Balboa who first sighted the Pacific and after Balboa the fierce, proud, ill-fated Magellan who first crossed the Pacific from east to west, in his circumnavigation of the world. Between the voyages of Columbus and Magellan there is only thirty years so that two oceans were taken in the space of three decades—such was the rush of exploration. Balboa sighted the Pacific in 1513. Magellan, rounding the South American continent, had sailed across it eight years later. England's Sir Francis Drake followed Magellan and soon the great ocean world of the Pacific was

8

opened to Europeans and being explored by Spanish, French, English and Dutch navigators.

But it was too vast to be fully known and the instruments of the early navigators too inaccurate for reliable charting of the islands they sighted. Because of this, two hundred and fifty years elapsed after Magellan's voyage before the Pacific could be said to be adequately explored following the three voyages of Captain James Cook.

But even then, there was still one group of several hundred islands which were unknown. They were the Fijis. They seem fated to have remained in a kind of limbo long after more obscure islands had been found and their position charted.

They were sighted and lost again, sighted and lost, like fabled islands that rise out of the sea and then disappear. They hung, as it were, in the shadows of the past, unwilling to emerge into the new world of the white strangers. The Solomons, New Guinea and Borneo, the Philippines, the Marianas, the Society and Sandwich (Hawaiian) Islands—all these were discovered and their positions charted. But the Fijis remained in obscurity though the islanders of other groups, particularly the Tongans, told explorers about them.

The Dutch navigator, Abel Tasman, was the first European to sight the Fijis. In 1643, Tasman was instructed by the Council of India, the Supreme Council of what had then become the Dutch East Indies, to make a voyage of "discovery and exploration of the known and unknown South Land." He was given two ships, the *Heemskerch* and the *Zeehaen*. They were small, flat-bottomed trading brigs, one carrying sixty men and the other fifty. The "south land" Tasman was to discover was a theoretical continent geographers believed must exist in the southern Pacific.

Tasman sailed from Europe by way of the Cape of Good Hope, refitted at Madagascar and from there headed south. He found no land but only increasing cold and turned eastward again to discover a huge island which he called Van Dieman's land after the Dutch governor of Batavia. It is now called Tasmania.

He missed Australia which might have provided the south land he sought, and continuing eastward came on the coast of New Zealand—four or five centuries after it had been discovered and settled by the Polynesians. The natives killed three of his men and he left, headed north-northeast, breasting the south Equatorial current for by now European ships were becoming efficient sailing crafts.

His next landfall was the islands of Tonga and here he was well received and given food and water. From Tonga he turned northwest and on February 6, 1643 found his two little ships caught in a maze of coral reefs. He was in the middle of the hurricane season and there was no anchorage.

A blinding rain cascaded around the two vessels to be followed by a period of complete calm, and then threatening, blustery winds. To his left lay deep water but neither tide nor wind would permit him to get to it. Ahead lay a barrier of coral thirty miles long and he could not work around the ends of it. Tasman, thanking God for the shallow draft of his ships, decided to sail over the coral. He made the crossing safely, with only inches between his keel and the coral reef and got into deep water on the other side.

Visibility was still poor because of mist and rain. He sighted a few points of land, but could not determine whether these represented separate islands or were all part of the one island. He noted their position and then left, just in time, for he was hardly clear of the coral maze that surrounded them before he was caught in a hurricane.

He returned to Batavia where the authorities thought little of his explorations and for over a hundred years there was no further sighting of the Fiji Islands by explorers. Tasman's description of them, indeed, was enough to keep navigators away from their position. The Fijis seemed to be nothing but a network of coral reefs and thus a place to be avoided.

The next to touch at the Fijis, in his second voyage of discovery in the Pacific, was Captain James Cook. He called at Tonga and there heard of the Fijis, and probably met some Fijians, for parties of Fijians went at times in their great canoes to Tonga, and the Tongans in return visited Fiji.

What Cook heard of the Fijis convinced him that he should avoid them. He learned that between the Tonga Islands and the bigger islands of the Fijis is another group, the Lau Islands, with only narrow passes between them and networks of coral. He was advised to stay to the south in traveling westward and he did. But he still found one of the Fiji Islands on whose beaches were so many turtles that he called it Turtle Island. He landed, but the natives fled. He left presents of some nails, a knife and some medals and then went away. That was in the year 1774. Cook sighted no other islands of the Fiji group, passing, on the advice of the Tongans, to the south. The great Captain Cook, who explored more of the Pacific than any other man, left the Fijis untouched by Europeans.

On Cook's third voyage of exploration, three years later, he had a young lieutenant, William Bligh, sailing with him as master of one of his two ships. Again Cook landed at Tonga and again heard stories of the Fijis.

Cook's two ships, *Resolution* and *Discovery*, remained in Tongan waters for three months and Bligh had plenty of opportunities to talk to the Tongans. He was, at the time, twenty years of age. The stories he heard convinced him, as they seemed to have convinced Cook, that the Fijis were islands to avoid. The natives were warlike, divided into little tribes which were continually fighting each other. There was no great chieftain over them, no central government or widely organized society.

11

The islanders were voracious cannibals and it was their custom to eat anyone who was shipwrecked off their shores —partly because of love of human flesh and partly because they believed that the sea gods must be angry with shipwrecked men. They clubbed and ate woman and children of neighboring tribes if they strayed from their villages, strangled or buried alive the old and weak, and when a hut was built for a chieftain, a man was buried alive in the hole in which the main pole of the hut was set, forced to hold the base of the pole in his arms as he suffocated.

Twelve years later Bligh was compelled to put his scanty knowledge of the Fiji Islands to use. He had been sent to Tahiti in command of the *Bounty* to bring back breadfruit which were to be taken to the West Indies to provide an abundance of cheap food for the slaves of the sugar planters. (Breadfruit is now plentiful in the British West Indian Islands, so plentiful that a great deal of it goes to waste.

Leaving Tahiti after six months of collecting the young trees, he sailed for Tonga and anchored in Nomuka Roads, in the southern half of the group, to take on wood and water. From Nomuka he headed north and when he was in sight of Tofua Island his crew mutinied and Bligh, with eighteen loyal officers and men, was put in the ship's launch, an open boat twenty-three feet long, fitted with a dipping lugsail and rowing six oars, and cast adrift. He had seven pounds of bread and a gallon of water for each man, four cutlasses, a grapnel for an anchor, and his sextant and a watch for navigational instruments.

The launch landed at Tofua the next day, but the Tongans were now hostile and killed one man. To the north and a little east lay the Samoan Islands which had already been discovered and not quite due east and further off, Tahiti. But Bligh's open boat could not sail against wind and current to Tahiti and if he was aware of the position of the Samoan Islands, he decided against heading for them.

Bligh made the astounding decision to turn west and, running before wind and ocean current, head for the Dutch East Indies, thirty-six hundred miles away. His course lay through the fearful Fijis—the Cannibal Islands—where shipwrecked men were eaten because the sea gods were angry with them and because the natives esteemed, over all dishes, a hash of human flesh.

Chapter Three

BLIGH'S course to Timor lay a little to the north of west, magnetic. His boat was so low in the water that even a moderate sea would lap over the side and after estimating the time to run the thirty-six hundred miles to Timor, (he ruled out of his estimate any possibility of obtaining food supplies on the way) he figured that he could allow one ounce of bread per man per day. The bread was weighed out in a pair of balances contrived of coconut shells, enough bread exactly to balance a pistol ball being issued to each man daily. To help him, he had the trade winds which blow from twelve to twenty miles an hour in these latitudes, above all the equatorial current—the great communication highway, as it were, of the Pacific—and with the aid of these he sighted the first of the Fiji Islands only two days after leaving Tofua in the Tonga group. He noted the position of the island as carefully as he might, with watch and sextant, but gave it no name. He did not land. He knew the people to be cannibals.

Two days later, ten more islands loomed in sight. At noon of that day, skirting a large island on which he dared not land, two enormous double canoes chased his boat. The canoes, when sighted, were about two miles away and close to the land. They gained steadily and in an hour had reduced the distance to a mile and in two hours were only half a mile away and coming on fast under their big mat sails.

Fortunately for Bligh the water was fairly calm and the

wind astern. In calm water his boat could move more readily and a stern wind is the worst wind for a sailing canoe. With such a wind, canoes have a tendency to bury their bows in the water—slowing them down—and the two chasing Bligh took longer than they should in catching his launch.

Bligh knew that a change of wind would doom him. The canoes would be capable of fifteen or twenty miles an hour to the launch's five. About the middle of the afternoon, with the chase still on and the canoes gaining every minute, there was a heavy rain squall. The rain came down so thickly that the canoes disappeared and Bligh, who always kept a cool head, filled every receptacle aboard with fresh water. When the squall passed, the wind died and a flat calm settled on the ocean.

The men took to the oars, knowing their lives depended on their efforts. With six men at the oars, and twelve in the bottom of the boat so that the oarsmen could not get a proper purchase with their feet, they pulled away hour after hour. One of the canoes gave up the chase but the other kept on. The Fijians aboard were sculling the canoe with the huge steering oar manned by three men. They crept up steadily on the boat. Just before sunset they were close enough to open fire with bows and arrows. Some of the arrows hit the water close to the launch. They were about four feet long and tipped with barbs made from the tail of a stingray. The barbs were so constructed that they would break off in the wound.

The sudden tropical dark saved Bligh. When the sun set and a huge full moon appeared in the east, the canoe abandoned the chase. A little wind came up and the launch continued on its westerly course. Bligh was saved. His boat, however, had to pass right through the Fiji Group and he sighted on his left the principal island, Viti Levu, and on his right, the second largest island, Vanua Levu. (It is from Viti Levu that the group takes its name, the word Fiji being

15

an attempt at pronouncing Viti. Viti Levu means big Fiji. Vanua Levu means big place or big island.) Bligh kept on avoiding the islands and landing nowhere. He was glad when he was clear of them at last.

Cook had touched at one small island in the southern extremity of the Fiji group. Tasman had been entangled in the labyrinth of reefs in the northeast. Bligh sailed right through the center of the group, leaving by a western passage now named Bligh Water. He was therefore the real discoverer of the Fijis whose position he plotted with remarkable accuracy in view of the instruments he had to use. It took the *Bounty* mutiny to unfold the vast extent of the islands and for awhile they were known as Bligh's Islands.

More discoveries were to come soon. When the frigate *Pandora* was sent out to look for the *Bounty* mutineers, one of her officers was Lieutenant Hayward, who had been a midshipman under Bligh and who survived with him the terrible voyage to Timor. The *Pandora* stopped at Tahiti and found fourteen of the mutineers. Some of them had built a small schooner in which they were about to quit Tahiti to escape capture when the *Pandora* arrived. The schooner was seized and put under the command of an officer named Oliver.

Oliver's schooner was separated from the *Pandora* in a storm off Samoa and he decided, being short of food and water, to do what Bligh had done and run for the Dutch East Indies.

Because he was anxious to avoid the cannibals of the Fijis, he stayed more to the south than Bligh had done. He landed on one island, probably Matuku, and was, therefore, the first white man to land on the Fijis. To his surprise, the huge dark savages, with their magnificent stand of woolly hair, received him well. He spent five weeks with them but wrote nothing of his experiences.

Bligh himself had not finished with Fiji. The tremendous

16

group of splendid mountainous islands through which he had sailed for several days in the launch, fascinated him. Three years after the *Bounty* mutiny he again undertook the assignment of getting breadfruit from Tahiti and taking them to the West Indies as food for slaves. He was given the ship *Providence* and a tender, the *Assistance*, for the task, and this time had plenty of marines on board as a precaution against mutiny.

Leaving Tahiti with his breadfruit, he headed for the Fijis and plotted the position of many of the islands. He passed the tremendous peaks of Korobasabasaga on the southeast corner of Viti Levu which look like a cockscomb against the sky, and spent a total of six days sailing through the group. But fear prevented him from landing.

After Bligh several other ships passed through or near the Fijis without any landing being made. The French ships *La Recherche* and *L'Esperence* sighted Vatoa which had previously been sighted by Cook. Captain Barber in the *Arthur* entered the group and anchored off Viti Levu. He was attacked by canoes, two of his men were wounded by arrows and he was only able to beat off his attackers by using muskets and swivel guns.

The London Missionary Society ship *Duff* was caught in the islands on a voyage to China from Tahiti and ran on a reef in a sea as mild as a country pond. She was not holed and got away and her captain plotted more of the islands and some of the reefs.

The American ship *Ann and Hope*, returning from a voyage to Australia, touched at Kandavu but without contact with the people. The eighteenth century came to a close with the islands located and many of them charted.

It took a shipwreck to put Europeans and Fijians in contact with each other and to break through the wall of terror that surrounded the islands.

Chapter Four

IT was a ship called the *Argo* that first opened the mysteries of the Fiji Islands to the world. The first *Argo* of Greek mythology had sought the golden fleece. Its namesake found a golden fleece in Fiji, but by accident.

There were signs in the heavens to foretell to the Fijians the coming of the *Argo*, for a great comet streaked through the sky and was accompanied by a shower of falling stars shortly before her arrival. This heavenly display filled the Fijans with awe and may have saved the lives of some of the *Argo*'s people.

The *Argo* was no vessel of classical beauty. She was a work a day three-masted schooner, trading between the penal settlements in Australia and the China coast. She picked up what cargoes she could and carried them wherever a profit lay and early in the eighteen hundreds—the precise date is not known but the year was probably 1800 itself—the *Argo*, on a voyage from China with a cargo for Port Jackson, was caught in a typhoon, blown hundreds of miles off her course and with a vast comet streaking through the night sky, struck on Mbukatatanoa reefs east of the island of Lakemba in the Fijis.

The reef is exposed to the open ocean and when there is any wind a tremendous swell pounds on its coral. The *Argo* was a total wreck in a matter of hours. Most of the crew were drowned or torn to death by the surf pounding them on the reef as they struggled in the water. A few of them were taken off by Fijians in canoes from nearby Oneata Island. Some died ashore and some survived.

The survivors were held in great awe for not only had their ship struck at the time of a comet but shortly after the shipwreck there was an astonishing hailstorm, pellets of ice flinging down from the tropical sky so that the Fijians believed the whites were gods able to summon the stars to their protection. They had never seen hailstones before, and thought them stars.

Ashore, the survivors of the *Argo* discovered a land of fearful wonders. They found magnificent huts whose ridge poles were the trunks of coconut palms and whose roofs, thatched with pandanus, plunged sharply to the ground and were twice as tall as the walls. They found villages grimly contained behind war fences of bamboo and coconut, and warriors who painted their faces in red and white and green according to whether they fought with club or spear or bow and arrow.

They discovered a people who were outrageous savages, yet kind and even gentle. A mother nursing her baby and crooning with content over it would pick up the roasted arm of a dead child to make a meal and offer her visitors a bite. Men thought it their duty to strangle or bury alive their aged parents and if a boy was seriously injured he was instantly clubbed to death for the Fijians believed firmly in an afterlife and maintained that all entered the next world in the same condition in which they left this one. A boy, then, who had lost a foot to a shark, should, in their belief, be killed immediately as a matter of mercy lest, handicapped, he suffer even greater injury before he died and be condemned to spend eternity minus not only a foot but perhaps an arm or a leg.

The names of the survivors of the *Argo* wreck have almost all been lost. A generation or two ago the Fijians of Mbau spoke of a white man who lived among them and was

19

SIERRA MADRE
PUBLIC LIBRARY
SIERRA MADRE
CALIFORNIA

called Na Matai—the craftsman. He was probably one of the seamen from the *Argo* who made his way to Mbau and who, like all seamen of his time, was skilled with tools. The islanders cherished him.

Another survivor was Oliver Slater and it was he who discovered the golden fleece of Fiji and brought the white men to the islands, overcoming their fears in their desire for riches.

Slater managed to get to the island of Vanua Levu. There he found growing along the shore thickets of a tree which he recognized immediately. He had been long enough in the China trade so he knew the trees were sandalwood. One grove of it represented a fortune for sandalwood was so valued by the Chinese that they even saved the sawdust.

The Fijians used the wood for scenting the coconut oil with which they anointed themselves. The area in which Slater made his discovery was to become known as The Sandalwood Coast.

About a year after Slater got ashore from the wreck of the *Argo*, the ship, *El Plumier*, cruising north-northwest from Tonga, came to anchor off Vanua Levu. Slater, ragged, bearded, suntanned, but now a person of some importance among the Fijians and with a good working knowledge of their language and customs, was paddled out to her in a canoe. He seemed mad, or at least deranged. He wanted a private interview with the captain, which he got, and babbled to him the story of the groves of sandalwood—whole forests of trees of gold—growing on the island.

But the captain of *El Plumier* had been long at sea, the ship had lost part of its keel and its rudder on a reef, and he was not interested in sandalwood. Then his crew, which had been on short rations, mutinied and seized the ship. They had heard of the sandalwood, for Slater did not keep his secret well. They cut some, repaired the ship, and headed for the China coast. Slater went with them but later made his way to Port

Jackson in Australia. Soon the capital of the Australian penal colony was buzzing with news of the discovery of sandalwood in the Fijis. Every ship that came there planned immediately to get to Fiji for a precious cargo which in China was worth about four hundred dollars a ton. One ship cleared a profit of a hundred thousand dollars from a single cargo—sufficient from one voyage for her captain to retire and live in luxury for the rest of his life.

Fiji's days of isolation were now over. Ships, heavily armed and laden with cheap trade goods, crowded into Sandalwood Bay on Vanua Levu loading cargoes of sandalwood. The trade, however, was hazardous—for a time perhaps the most hazardous that merchant ships have ever engaged in.

A terrible mesh of reefs surrounded the Fijis and they were uncharted. Some of these reefs thrust unexpectedly from a depth of two thousand fathoms to the surface of the ocean and even today's depth-sounding equipment is useless in dealing with such a hazard. Unknown currents swept around the islands to carry a ship becalmed up on the reefs and the immense depth on the seaward side made it impossible for those aboard to save themselves by dropping an anchor.

Men who sailed from Port Jackson looking for a fortune from a single voyage could expect to find, as an alternative, death by drowning or death by Fijian war clubs. Knowing the hazards, shipowners cynically weighted the scales against the ship's crews. Only the oldest vessels were sent to Fiji to pick up sandalwood. The *Argo* was the first of the wrecks but there were many to follow and few survivors to tell the tale. And yet the profits from a successful voyage were so enormous that soon ships were sailing for the Fijis from ports as far off as New England and India.

Sandalwood (*santalum yasi*) is a root parasite which thrives on the roots of other trees. The voracious demand for cargoes of sandalwood was such that twelve years after Slater got to Australia with his news, every stick of the wood was ripped off the Sandalwood Coast and ships that had been able to take aboard cargoes of several hundred tons in a matter of weeks were soon spending months getting a cargo of a few hundred pounds.

Technically no vessel could clear from Port Jackson, Australia, to engage in the sandalwood trade without the permission of the governor of the colony who at the time was Captain William Bligh, the same man who had survived the *Bounty* mutiny. The British government, having failed to save the East India Company by shipping tea to the American colonies, was still intent on doing its best to preserve it. Exclusive trading rights had then been granted with this object to the East India Company over most of what was called the South Seas. An Act of Parliament forbade British whalers from chasing whales further north than the equator or further east than the 241st meridian. As a result American merchant ships and American whalers, who were not tender over the prosperity of the East India Company, soon monopolized whaling in the North and South Pacific—and the sandalwood trade as well.

British shipowners, to overcome the handicap, engaged in a practice that lay somewhere between piracy and smuggling. They applied in Port Jackson for clearance papers for China, India, London or any port or place that seemed plausible, sailed away, and as soon as they were over the horizon, trimmed their yards for the Sandalwood Coast in Fiji.

Within six years of the wreck of the *Argo*, the Sandalwood Coast was the best known port in the Pacific. It was no port, as such, but just a bay behind a coral reef in which ships from Australia, New England, India, the Dutch East Indies and France swung at anchor while their captains dickered ashore for cargoes of sandalwood. Culturally, Fiji was in the Stone Age and the trade goods brought by the ships were miserable. They consisted largely of chisels, nails, beads and ax heads fashioned by the ship's blacksmith out of soft iron during the voyage. The East Indiamen had one advantage in the trade. They brought elephant tusks as trade goods and soon learned that among the Fijians the most prized possession was a whale's tooth. Elephant tusks, then, were cut up on board into small pieces and carved by the ship's carpenter to look like the tooth of a sperm whale, when they were traded to the Fijians for precious sandalwood.

There was a touch of blasphemy in this deceit for among the Fijians a whale's tooth has a mystical and sacred nature. Even today the greatest gift the Fijian can bestow on any-one—and it is always given for great public service and nobility of character—is a *tanoa*, a whale's tooth. In their first contacts with the whites the Fijians then were the victims of a kind of spiritual fraud.

As the supplies of sandalwood dimished, the traders started currying favor with petty chiefs to obtain what remained, and for a few hundred pounds of wood, would join them in their wars against other tribes.

The Fijis had been a place of war before the arrival of Europeans. But these wars were small and it was not unusual for a chief, intending to raid another's village, to send a herald to warn him. Massive butcheries were not common and in most of these wars only a few hundred warriors were engaged. The sandalwood traders changed this.

The chief of Mbua, which is the capital of the Sandalwood Coast, was at the time a man called Rawaike. He was not reckoned a very powerful chief among the islanders, but be-cause of the trade, he soon became tremendously prosperous. Seeking his favor, the captain of one vessel built him a wooden house, the first wooden house erected in the Fijis. Other chieftains became jealous of his wealth and position and plotted against him. The sandalwood traders backed Rawaike to retain his favor and soon boat crews armed with muskets and cutlasses were joining the warriors of Rawaike in attacks on neighboring chieftains.

Muskets did terrible work among the natives. The Fijians could not understand the weapon and saw no connection between the noise and smoke of the discharge and a man falling dead or mutilated by buckshot some distance off. They thought, for awhile, that the white men had magical powers of killing, and whites who jumped ship to live ashore were in great demand among the native chiefs.

Some of these men, despite the hard standards of their day and the brutalities of life at sea, were decent men. But the greater number were the worst of white society. Ship's captains, short of a crew and bound for the Fijis, helped convicts in the penal settlements in Australia to escape and shipped them on board as seamen. Many of these men proved so useless on board ship that they were marooned in the Fijis. Others jumped ship to become beachcombers. The first of the whites to live ashore among the Fijians were desperate men, outcasts among their own people, and so degenerate and cruel that many became outcasts even among the cannibals of Fiji. But it was from these that the Fijians got their first impression of the *papalangi*, the white men.

One of the better sort to live among the Fijians was a Scotsman, William Lockerby, who was a mate on the American ship *Jenny* when it called at Mbua Bay (the Sandalwood Coast) in 1808 to pick up a cargo. By this time the sandalwood had largely gone from the area and Lockerby was ordered by his captain to go further up the coast and see if he could locate new supplies.

Lockerby had not been getting along well with his captain and returning to Mbua Bay after many adventures, found that the *Jenny* had sailed and he was marooned ashore. He turned for protection to the Fijian chieftain who treated him kindly. When food was short the chieftain made sure that Lockerby did not starve and he advised Lockerby to win the approval of the tribesmen by dressing as they did. Accordingly, Lockerby lived ashore with the Fijians with only a belt around his waist made from the bark of a tree in the way of clothes, and he painted his hair black and at other times red.

Lockerby was the first European really to understand the Fijians. He became genuinely fond of them, finding them kind and gentle. But he could not stomach their cannibalism and was horrified time and again by their offers of dishes of human flesh. Once he witnessed the strangling of an elderly woman who, it had been decided, was too old to be allowed to live further. He tried to save the woman's life by offering a whale's tooth for her.

"Keep your whale's tooth," said the chieftain misunderstanding him. "This woman is too old to be of any use to you. If you want a woman we have many young ones from whom you may take your pick."

Lockerby was unable to convince the chief that it was from mercy and for no other reason that he wished the woman to be spared. But the Fijians did not understand this kind of mercy. The woman would be reborn in another world immediately after death, at her present age. To let her live further would be to condemn her to an eternity of senility. She was strangled out of pity and Lockerby was compelled to witness this ritual killing.

At these stranglings the friends of the victim assisted. The cord was passed around the throat and pulled tight and the friends of the victim pushed his or her head forward and held it down to hasten death which came in a matter of a few minutes.

The mental attitude of these voluntary victims of strangulation seems, on a close examination, to have been fear of continuing to live rather than pleasure at the thought of death. When a chief died, his favorite wives were strangled to accompany him in the other world.

Some of the early missionaries who did their best to stamp out this practice spoke to many strangulation victims whom they offered to save but found the women too ashamed to continue to live after their husbands were dead. Their friends expected them to die, even their closest friends. The whole tribe expected them to submit to strangulation. Life, as they saw it, would be intolerable both from the nagging of their own consciences and the scorn of their companions if they refused death. So they submitted to the strangler's cord, some of them dressing themselves in their own funeral robes, anointing themselves for death, and just before dying, making a pretense of unconcern by wishing their friends, who gathered around them, good crops, good fishing, plenty of children and all the fruits of the earth from which they were about to depart forever.

The strangulation custom had a tragic effect upon children. If the father died, either by natural causes or was killed in battle, then the mother had to die, too, and her children were witnesses to her death. They were left orphans. When the sandalwood wars started, Fiji villages were full of orphans whose fathers had been killed and whose mothers had been strangled. Some of these children survived in the villages, taken care of by others. But many, straying from their villages, were clubbed and eaten by other tribesmen.

The Fijians were and still are tremendously fond of children. There is a story told of one woman who for the good of her child decided to send it to Tonga where it would be safe from the frightful butchery in which the Fijis were then plunged. The child was put on a ship and the mother stayed with her until the ship had drawn away from the reef. She was then made to jump overboard and swim to a canoe which was to take her ashore. She jumped into the sea but instead of heading for the canoe tried to swim after the ship and as it pulled away, stopped swimming through exhaustion. The people in the canoe found her and pulled her on board and she denounced them as false friends who would save her life now that her child was gone from her.

Over newly born children, however, Fijian mothers were

26

not so tender. Newborn girls were often suffocated by their mothers who pinched the nostrils together and put their hands over the mouths to achieve this.

The strangulation victims and babies killed at birth were never eaten. They were buried even in time of famine. In Fijian cannibalism there was a measure of hate and revenge, though the whole motivation behind the custom is still not fully explained. Beyond a doubt, human flesh was enjoyed as a food, and particularly when served in the form of a hash. But when a man had killed his enemy he very quickly cut out his tongue and his liver and heart and ate with the relish of hatred.

The Fijians had a tremendous ability for hate and could bide their time over a period of twenty years or more to achieve vengeance. Like the knights of the feudal period in Europe, who would abstain from certain foods or shave their heads until some wrong had been righted, the Fijian would swear not to eat a certain vegetable or not to speak a word until some enemy had been killed.

One spent ten years of his life replying to questions by whistling until a man who had injured him was killed when, having eaten the man's tongue, he spoke his first words in a decade.

When the wars, instigated to no small extent by the sandalwood trade, grew in intensity there were terrible scenes of carnage as the European musket was allied with the ferocity of the islanders. Lockerby, shortly before he escaped from the islands, saw a fleet of canoes returning from a raid, their decks piled with corpses and captives. There not being sufficient room on the decks of the canoes to carry all the human booty, captive children were hauled in baskets to the tops of the masts where they were beaten to death as the baskets crashed into the mast with every wave. After such a raid there would be a tremendous cannibal feast which turned the stomachs of even the worst of the white beach-

27

combers. This, however, did not prevent them from taking part in and even promoting tribal wars.

War and sandalwood went together. When the Fijians awakened to the value of the sandalwood thickets, although they had previously had little regard for the possession of particular pieces of territory, they began to lay claim to areas known to contain sandalwood.

Tribes that had lived in comparative peace side by side fought horribly for possession of a few acres. They fought, too, to obtain the soft-iron chisels and nails and medals and muskets which were the gifts of the Europeans and were great wonders among them. It was not long before a chieftain would tell a ship's captain that before any sandalwood could be supplied, the ship's crew must help attack a neighboring tribe.

The sandalwood traders had no compunction about this and one, following such a raid, noted in his journal that to get sandalwood he assisted the Waileas to destroy their enemies who were cut up, baked, and eaten in his presence. He then got his sandalwood.

As the supplies of the wood petered out the sandalwood traders were required to help more and more in these wars. Thirty years after the end of the trade, whole sections of the coast of Vanua Levu, previously heavily populated, were utterly deserted. The adults had been killed and eaten and those of the children who survived, died by accident or starvation.

Despite these horrors and terrors there was soon a score of worthless whites living ashore in Vanua Levu as part of the retinue of some tribal chief. William Diapea, who was known as Cannibal Jack, had three wives and set himself up as a trader and gunsmith. He collected turtle shell and Bêche-de-Mer and mended the old Tower muskets which were soon the super weapon of the Fiji wars.

Another, Paddy Connor or Connell, was an escaped convict from Australia who became a kind of court jester to the chief of Rewa on Viti Levu. He lived until around the middle of the nineteenth century, for he had a quick mind with which to defend himself, though his morals disgusted Fijian and white men alike. Before he died he had a hundred wives and he confessed in his old age that his ambition was to father fifty children. Unfortunately it is not known whether he achieved this ambition.

Chapter Five

I WENT to Fiji by impulse rather than design. I was on my way from California to Australia and the ship touching at Suva on Viti Levu, I decided to leave it there. The name Suva had a wild attraction for me and the mountains that surround the bay a savage, adventurous look which immediately brought to my mind the great days of American whaling and Melville's South Seas.

I knew nothing of the Fijis. Landing in Suva I smelled the musty scent of copra, saw piled outside a warehouse hills of trochus shell from which shirt buttons are made, saw around me a splendid dark-skinned people whose bushy hair was combed upward in pride and who carried themselves with the grace of lions. And so I knew I had come to the right place and was so fascinated by the islands that I returned again and will once more, for in Fiji I found something rare—a native people living in their native ways, building their houses of pandanus thatch as they have done for thousands of years, fishing off the reefs in outriggers, and retaining, not for tourists but for themselves, their splendid ceremonials.

Fiji is greatly changed from the days of the sandalwood traders. Cannibalism is gone but the people have the grace not to be overly ashamed of it. They are Christians, as good as you will find anywhere in the world, and perhaps better. Christianity is not a yoke about their necks but a flowering of a kind and generous spirit which even in the worst days of Fiji their unkindest judges found among them.

30

Approach one of their villages in which they live in houses of thatch and you are met, though a stranger, with smiles not of politeness but of welcome. You are hardly there before you are taken to the chief or *buli's bure* and sitting upon a floor covered by a pandanus mat, are offered a bowl of *yangona*—a narcotic drink called *kava* in the Polynesian islands and *ava* in the Hawaiian Islands.

The drink is always prepared fresh and is served even on informal occasions with a little ceremony. It is offered you by a cup bearer who kneels before you and with arms outstretched, hands you the polished half coconut shell called a *bilo* full of *yangona*.

You must drink it down without pause and when you have done, all the Fijians present clap their hands in cadence and you return the bowl with the word *vinaka* which means "good."

In Fiji the people are dark skinned, handsome, well made and easy with themselves. There is no color problem for they have always had a pride in their race. They are secure in their heritage, cherishing their own dances, styles of hairdress and legends. They speak their own language and on some of the islands nothing else, so that in my travels around I needed an interpreter or failing one had to converse by sign language. Yet at no time was I made to feel embarrassed and at no time did any one of the Fijians attempt to make a profit from me. It was difficult to pay for anything in the remoter islands, and Fijians whom I had known only a day or two got up at dawn to see me off and said farewell as if parting with a dear friend.

All this would seem to be in sharp contrast to their fearful past. Yet the truth is that the Fijian, despite his reputation, had always a great measure of generosity and kindness. The cannibals were, in fact, kindly.

When I landed in Suva I knew no one and had not even a lodging for the night. But I had soon met the chief of the

Fiji Visitor's Bureau, Don Lane, who installed me at the Grand Pacific Hotel of which one wing would not be out of place in Beverly Hills and the other would be familiar to travelers in the middle years of Queen Victoria. The older part is all polished wood, high-ceilinged rooms, and potted palms and is as charming and restful a place as a man could wish. I was not long in the hotel before I had met a giant Fijian from the eastern island of Kambara in the Lau Group. His name was Ned. He was dressed in a red shirt and gray *sulu* or wraparound Fijian skirt worn by men. His hair was combed upwards in an imposing crown so that several inches were added to his six-foot-four. When I stood beside him I felt like a child and he was soon telling me of Kambara and the *yangona* bowls which are carved there with a hand chisel from a single block of wood with no means of measurement other than the eye.

"You must go to Kambara," he said. "There you will find our people living in their old ways. They will be glad to see you." I determined that I would.

The Grand Pacific Hotel faces the main road out of Suva and its rear parallels the sea coast with a large lawn of coarse buffalo grass leading to the seawall. I had fallen in love with Suva Bay with its splendid backdrop of mountains among which one peak sticks up like a giant's thumb. This peak is the solidified flux of an old volcanic cone for the islands are volcanic. The cone has eroded, leaving only the solid amalgam which once filled it.

On my first day I took a walk along the seawall, enjoying the lovely bay which has about it the silence of the centuries, and my eye was attracted to something that moved at my feet. I looked down and saw to my horror a snake, banded elegantly in black-and-white rings. It was crawling along the sloping wall quite slowly, every now and then thrusting its small head into a crevice. I rushed back to find Ned and brought him to see the snake. He smiled, bent down, reached out a hand as big as a nail keg, grabbed the snake whose head was in a crevice, and pulled it out. It writhed, though not vigorously, in his huge fist.

"*Dadakalavi*," he said.

"Is it poisonous?" I asked.

"It is quite harmless," said Ned. "There are many of them about. The children going to school sometimes tie them around their necks for ties." He offered me the snake but I have an abiding distrust of them and would not take it. Later I learned that *dadakalavi* has a virulent poison but unlike land snakes the poison is in the rear teeth of the tiny mouth.

The head of this specimen was no bigger than a bean and the snakes are not vicious or aggressive but feed only on fish and crabs. Big ones, two or three feet in length, have been caught and on being hung up by their tails to the branch of a tree, disgorge the fish they have eaten which are swallowed whole. I never did this myself but in swimming off the island of Nukulau with a party of children saw several sea snakes which passed among us, the children crying with delight and splashing and chasing them.

In Fiji even the snakes are friendly. Later I picked up one of these handsomely banded sea serpents myself. Though I gripped it tight, it was able to writhe out of my fist. The skin felt rough, like sandpaper.

There were at one time, and there may still be, large constrictor snakes in the Fiji Islands. They reached the islands before the first human immigrants and this may account for the old Fijian belief that the supreme deity was a huge serpent, Ndengei, who lived in a cave in the northeast end of Viti Levu but did not much concern himself with human affairs. Perhaps the first men to arrive in canoes which sail-drifted to the islands found huge boas already there and assumed that these were gods.

The snakes followed the same route from Southeast Asia as that taken by the pioneer Melanesians. They were brought

33

on impromptu rafts—tangles of trees and vines swept down the rivers at flood time—driven by the same great currents that brought the first human migrants to the islands. Constrictor snakes (and indeed snakes generally) are able to go for astonishing periods without taking food. And so the big boas could spend two or more months on these rafts until thinned and glistening with sea salt, they reached the Fijis when they writhed ashore to inhabit the islands.

Rob Wright, who is official photographer of the Fiji government, told me that once, visiting the island of Nukulau which lies only a short distance from Suva, one of the islanders told him that there was a big snake in a clump of trees nearby. No one had ever heard of a snake on Nukulau and he did not believe the story, but went anyway to see what had excited the islander. There, in the thicket of trees, lay a huge constrictor snake. It could only have come by sea from the Asiatic mainland; an involuntary voyager on a raft of driftwood, repeating, in this century, a journey first made millions of years ago.

Rob Wright took me under his wing when we first met and introduced me to the wonders of Fiji, not I think out of any desire to publicize the islands, but because he wanted to share their delights with me. We have been firm friends ever since. The day after my arrival he called me at the Grand Pacific Hotel and I went over to his office to introduce myself. We were, we soon discovered, both divers and I had brought some gear with me, hoping to dive off the Great Barrier Reef in Australia.

"The diving off Viti Levu is not particularly good," said Rob. "But we have a reef in the Fijis which is something like the Great Barrier Reef. Not anywhere near so big, of course, but with as many submarine curiosities. It is called the Great Astrolabe."

"Is it possible to dive on it?"

"We would have to get a boat..."

34

"Let's get a boat. Could you come?"

Although he had known me only an hour or so, Rob said he could. And so we chartered the power boat *Sere-na-Wai*, which means "Song of the Sea," and joined by Bud Rose of the Royal New Zealand Air Force, who supplied me with air tanks, headed for the Great Astrolabe Reef.

The reef lies east of the island of Kandavu. It is one of the terrible guardian reefs that surround most of the hundreds of islands of the Fijis which cover an ocean area of an hundred thousand square miles. But that area is only a drop, as it were, in the vastness of the Pacific.

The voyage to the Great Astrolabe Reef was my first intimate acquaintance with the tropical South Seas. On a liner one is as remote from the ocean as, living in a hotel, one is remote from the flowers and lawns around. Liners protect their passengers from the ocean and with their array of shops and hairdressers and tailors and dining rooms and ballrooms, foster the pretense that the ocean is not really there. On deck, the passenger is thirty or forty feet above the surface of the water and cannot feel the ocean.

But once in the *Sere-na-Wai*, the ocean was only three or four feet from us and utterly splendid. It was all azure and argent, the colors of heraldry; an immense world of blue, quick and lively, stretching to an infinity to which the gateway was the ever-receding horizon.

The splendid ocean rhythms made themselves felt, long, low, powerful tollers which, from trough to trough, might measure two hundred yards and whose gently inclined sides lifted the *Sere-na-Wai* ten or fifteen lazy feet to drop her easily down on the other side the same lulling distance.

There were other waves, moving over these at an angle, and caused by the fresh trade wind, and others, of which I was not then aware, caused by the deflection of the water around reefs or distant islets.

These wave patterns were used by the early Fijians and

indeed all the islanders of the South Pacific, to find their way from island to island, though this ancient navigation is now almost lost, killed by the compass. It still exists, I am told, in the Marshall Islands, but is not likely to survive many more generations. A hundred or more miles from the nearest land, the islander lies on his back in the bottom of his canoe and listens to the sound of the waves on the hull. He listens carefully, for the sound pattern of the waves is the basis of his art. He knows the pattern and the direction from which they come and uses two sets of waves, coming from differing directions, to get a fix on his position, as others use signals from radio beacons. He knows that these two sets of waves, when they meet land, are bent and deflected from their normal course.

Lying and listening in the bottom of the canoe he waits until he can sense this bend in the direction of the waves. Then he picks the point where the waves meet each other and, using this as his bearing, follows it and so arrives unerringly at the island that brought about the interruption of the waves' patterns.

This navigational art was handed down in the islands from generation to generation, and stick charts were constructed showing islands and the wave pattern around them. But during the Second World War, thousands of compasses were issued to the islanders in return for their aid to the Allies. The younger people preferred to rely on the compass than go through the long course of training required to master their older form of navigation. So the art dwindles and may soon be lost for it is not something that can be written down and thus mastered. It is a skill that has to be learned through feeling and if one generation is skipped, it will be gone forever.

The distance from Suva to the Great Astrolabe Reef is not great. We left about two in the morning and arrived shortly before noon when I got my first view of a great tropical coral reef. On one side the water was an intense blue so that dipping my hand in it, I was surprised that it was not stained blue when I drew it out. A frosted silver line marked the top of the reef and beyond it the water was pure emerald. On the ocean side the reef plunged down to the bottom seven and eight thousand feet below. On the landward side were great coral gardens in which it was possible to stand in water at places only four foot deep.

The reef is an example of the ship traps that are scattered through the Fijis. They lie thickest in the northeast corner of the group and no depth-sounding equipment will safeguard a ship threading its way through them, for the depths range from thousands of feet to nothing in a matter of a cable length. Untold numbers of ships have been lost on these reefs, some known and some unknown.

The Great Astrolabe itself is named after a French corvette which was nearly wrecked on it.

On the way over Rob, who loves to fish, trolled a line behind the *Sere-na-Wai* and had soon hooked a fine albacore. But hardly had the fish struck before the dorsal fins of two sharks appeared lancing through the water.

"We will meet plenty of them when we dive," said Rob. reeling the fish in fast as the sharks headed for it.

I rather looked forward to doing so, for I had never dived among sharks before.

Chapter Six

NOBODY knows how far down the coral reefs go that surround almost all the Fiji Islands. They extend far beyond diving depth. Some believe that they commence on the bottom and come up through several thousand feet. Others hold that the polyps, whose chalky skeletons form the coral, commenced their building on submarine peaks and ridges of volcanic origin and so the coral does not extend more than a few hundred feet below the surface, the rest being rock. It will be possible to answer the question with certainty only when divers can go down to depths of six and seven thousand feet and move about with ease.

Diving over the top of a reef like the Great Astrolabe is like jumping over the lip of the Grand Canyon. At one moment you are standing uncertainly on the edge overweighted by your diving gear, or perhaps swimming on the surface of the sea with the writhing hard coral masses only a few inches from your faceplate. A second later and you are in space, suspended in the midair of the ocean, unable to see bottom.

You immediately become dizzy and fearful and tend to reach out for the wall of the reef lest you plunge to the bottom. It takes a little effort of mind to recall that you are floating and will not fall into the depths. You go down, as I did with Rob, past massive outcrops of brain coral and others of staghorn which is poisonous and inflicts a festering wound if touched, and as you descend there is no perceptible change in the light.

The sunlight strikes down from above, illuminating the top

of the coral outcrops, shedding light like a cascade of satin down the side of the reef, and leaving the underparts in dark and nervous shadows. There is, as always, the sense of being watched so that you are distracted between the peacock display of a sea worm, its tentacles of dark green thrust out of the tubular sheath in which it lives, and the desire to look behind and below and above you for "the watchers." They are all around, silent, coldly observant and invisible.

The ocean itself watches you. Look up and you see above a sky of living silver, all quivering with life—the surface. Look out from the reef and you lose your balance, for out there all is blue and you are suspended in space and staring at infinity. Look down and the reef slips deeper and deeper with here and there a giant's head of coral thrust out until all disappears into blue nothingness.

And then, out of the blue nothingness below, something emerges. At first it is nothing more than a thread of darkness in the blue and then it becomes a form like a dull leaf distantly observed and then it becomes a long brown fish. And then it becomes a shark.

The first I saw appeared in this manner, far, far below. It floated rather than swam toward us and its speed was astonishing for in less than a minute it had reached our level and, making a graceful banking turning in the blue, came in on us with eyes like those of an executioner examining the condemned. The head of a shark, closely observed, is remarkably like a front view of a nineteenth-century coffin when the box was shaped to come in from the shoulders about the head of the corpse. The nose forms a distinct ridge from which the snout slips back to a mouth like a sickle or a crescent moon.

The eyes are of gray steel and the pectoral fins held stiffly out like the wings of a fighter jet. The shark, which had floated so swiftly up from the depths, inched in on Rob who was ahead of me until Rob could have reached out with his spear gun and touched it on the snout. Then, without any but the

39

laziest of movements, the shark glided off to make another circle and come in for a further examination.

This was the first of perhaps half a dozen sharks we met off the Great Astrolabe Reef in twenty minutes of diving. They were as thick as horseflies in a stable, all blacktips or whitetips and all hunting. Yet none attacked, though the same species are so voracious in the Solomons, not many miles to the northeast of the Fijis, that you dare not get into the water— even shallow water behind a reef. There is a well-authenticated story of a visitor to the Solomons, picnicking with his wife and children in a launch, who decided to combat the heat of the day by going for a swim. He had hardly slipped over the side of the boat when he let out a great cry. The water was immediately scarlet with blood and all that was recovered of him were his hands of which his wife had got hold.

The islanders of the Solomons are often attacked in their canoes by sharks. The sharks will rush at the canoe and bite the sides, leaving a whole set of teeth embedded in the wood. Behind each set of teeth in a shark's mouth, are series of other sets, which move forward to take the place of those lost in this manner. That the same species of shark in the Fijis did not attack us suggests that sharks spend their lives in the neighborhood in which they are born and in which they develop particular feeding habits. The man-eaters of the Solomons have fed for countless generations on human flesh for it was the practice of the islanders in pre-Christian days to dispose of their dead by leaving their bodies on reefs for the sharks. They have thus developed a taste for human flesh.

The Fijians have little fear of sharks and if attacked will often fight a shark rather than try to escape. There is a man in Suva minus both hands—the result of a fight with a shark. The shark attacked and he was so enraged that he grabbed it and managed, though bitten, to drag the creature onto the top of a reef. There, outraged at being attacked, he beat the shark on the head with his fists. The shark snapped and took the man's hands off.

Another Fijian, hearing a woman shout in the water, dashed in to save her though there was blood all around. She shouted to him to go back, for she was already dying. The Fijian went on, however, beat the shark off and dragged the woman ashore where she died from her terrible wounds.

One of the early missionaries to Fiji was a Tongan, Joel Bulu, who, wishing to swim across a river, waded into the ocean at its mouth. A shark attacked and took a bite out of his thigh. It circled and came back for more and Bulu, seeing the mouth open, thrust his hand down the maw, reaching as far in as he could. The shark closed its mouth, though not hard, and Bulu, highly enraged, worked his arm in further until the shark was choking and opened its jaws wide. Bulu withdrew his arm, now lacerated to the bone, and seized the shark around the gills, lifted it up and started in his rage to carry it ashore to kill it. He kept his head down for the shark was snapping its jaws above him and he was afraid of being bitten. He had almost got the shark ashore when his right arm lost all its strength and fell helpless to his side. The shark slipped into the water and tried to swim away. Bulu grabbed it with his left arm, seized the tail and tried to pull it back when he fell fainting into the water from loss of blood. The shark got away and Bulu was saved from drowning by his friends.

As for myself, after the day's diving we anchored for the night in the lagoon of an uninhabited island, Yaukuve. I saw little enough of the island that day for the sudden tropical night came on us when we entered the lagoon. But waking the next morning to the sound of sea birds, I found the *Sere-na-Wai* floating, as it were, on a liquid emerald. The lovely water was still and transparent so that in forty feet I could see individual shells in all their details on the bottom. I went ashore with Rob to explore.

No footprints marked the crescent of white beach on which

41

we landed. A hundred thousand shells lay strewn through the gleaming sand and ribbons of sea lace, more delicate than the filigree of Portugal, marked the high-tide level. Coconuts, the plantings of accident rather than design, rose gracefully out of the thick undergrowth that lined the glittering beach. Their fronds pattered in the wind and of other sounds there was only the lapping of wavelets on the shore and the distant sibilance of the surf on the reef.

On Yaukuve, as on some two hundred other islands and islets in the Fijis, not a soul lives. In the underbrush, beneath the palms, there were the remnants of a little hut built by Fiji fishermen who had spent the night there occasionally, but no other habitation was on the island. The beach was a slow crescent, terminating in two headlands of rock. The morning air was sparkling clear and over all lay a profound and reverend silence.

Yaukuve lies in a little tail of islets stringing out to the north of Kandavu. They all have a kind of magic to them as if they were islands of legend rather than geography. They gleam in the sun in emerald and gold, each with its fringe of silver surf about its glittering beaches. There are no towns, only villages on these islets, and the people live communally in the villages of thatched huts under their chiefs as they have done since time immemorial.

Of all these islands, perhaps the most magical is Kandavu itself. The island is long, lying roughly north and south, and in its center is a narrow isthmus so that you can climb to the top of a hill on the isthmus and look at the ocean on both sides. Long ago the warriors of Kandavu, wishing to pass from one side of the island to the other, rolled their outrigger canoes on logs up this hill and down the other side to save the sea journey around the island.

In the waters here, great turtles abound. You may come across them at sea, floating lazily on the surface, their tremendous shells looking as big as a door. The large ones weigh several hundred pounds and although elsewhere through the Fijis, turtles are fished for the shells are valuable and the meat as good as beefsteak, in Kandavu it is forbidden to take them, and that because the turtles are relatives of the villagers of Namuana.

"The women of Namuana gather at times on the cliffs overlooking the bay and sing to the turtles to call them out of the sea," said Rob. "I have heard them do it many times, and seen the turtles come up and lie in the water of the bay and listen to the singing."

"Tell me the story," I said.

"It is a legend," said Rob. "It is also, I believe, a piece of history—that is to say, it is a legend based on truth. In the old days when warfare was the principal sport of the men of Fiji, village fought village, and the villagers of Namuana on Kandavu were the enemies of the village of Nabukelevu nearby. There was nothing strange in this for this was the time of fear in Fiji, when women and children who strayed from their villages, were likely to be seized and eaten by the warriors of another village.

"The wife of the big chief of Namuana was a beautiful woman named Tinaicabonga. I do not know what the name means. It could mean the woman who speaks sharply, that is, with authority, or the woman who is set apart or dedicated, but all agree that she was very beautiful. She had a daughter Raudalice to whom she was devoted and the two often went fishing together on a reef.

"One day they went further than usual in their fishing and waded out to a reef at the eastern end of the bay. They were so busy that they did not notice the approach of a great war canoe from Nabukelevu. The warriors on the canoe seized the two women, bound them hand and foot with vines and tossed them into the bottom of the canoe. The women knew they were to be killed and eaten and pleaded for their lives but without effect.

43

"The women then prayed to their gods to save them and the gods were kind and prevented the canoe moving through the water. However hard the warriors paddled, their canoe went no further. Again the women asked to be freed but the warriors were unimpressed and refused. They prayed again and the sea god, pitying them, caused a storm to arise. Foam-crested rollers rushed on the canoe from all sides. The waves brought down the mast and sail and swamped the vessel. Water filled the bottom of the canoe where the two women were lying and the warriors, anxious to save themselves, left them there to drown.

"One, however, glanced at the two captives and found that they had changed into sea turtles. He shouted to the others and they picked up the two turtles and put them into the ocean. The sea was immediately calm and the turtles swam away.

"When the chief and tribesmen of Namuana heard what had happened to the princess and her daughter, all the maidens of the village assembled on the cliff tops to sing a song of mourning. As they were singing the princess and her daughter, now in the form of turtles, swam to the surface to listen to them. Every time the women have sung since that day the turtles have reappeared. There are now not two but dozens of turtles that respond to the singing. The ceremony is a very solemn one, no smiling or laughter is permitted and only the women from the village of Namuana may be present. If any of the women of Nabukelevu join the singers, the turtles will not appear."

"What is the song they sing?" I asked.

"In English it goes like this," said Rob.

" 'The women of Namuana are all dressed in mourning

'Each carries a sacred war club, each is tattooed in a strange pattern

'Do rise to the surface Raudalice so we may look at you

'Rise to the surface Tinaicabonga so we may see you also.' "

"Is all this true?" I asked.

"Yes," said Rob quickly. "It is true. There are many things in Fiji like that."

To the north of Kandavu lies the island of Ono which is part of a little tail of islands streaming out from Kandavu. These islands came into being as the result of a quarrel between two gods. Both gods lived on Kandavu, one at one end and the other at the other end. One of them, Molau, was the owner of the huge mountain of Nabukelevu. The gods were friends and often drank *kava* together. The second god, whose name was Tanovo, was envious of the huge mountain of Nabukelevu, and thought he would like to get some of it to make a few islands for himself.

One day while the two were drinking *kava* and Molau had fallen asleep, Tanovo filled two huge baskets with rock and earth from the mountain, slung them on a pole over his shoulder and started off with them.

His friend Molau woke up and chased him clear off the end of Kandavu. Tanovo fell into the water and the contents of one basket became the island of Ono and the earth and rock from the other basket was scattered over the water to form the other islets. It is because they were made by gods perhaps that these islands have a magical quality to them.

I wanted to go with Rob in the *Sere-na-Wai* to see the women charm the turtles to the surface of the sea with their singing, but the wind hauled around to the north and the weather looked unpromising and so we had to go back to Suva and leave Kandavu unvisited.

Later I made a second attempt to witness the calling of the turtles. Only two years had intervened but something very sad had happened.

The women still call the turtles but they charged a fee and

the fee was beyond my means. They had a magic and have turned it into profit. This is not their fault.

For centuries Fiji lived in its own way but then the world thrust itself upon it and, to cope with this world which came unbidden, magic is not enough. The people have to have money. That is the sadness.

Chapter Seven

TO the east of Viti Levu and toward the center of the Koro Sea around which the islands of Fiji are bent like the tail of a scorpion is the island of Nairai. Like all the Fiji Islands it has as its battlement a reef. Nairai's reef, however, was a reef of destiny for the whole of Fiji, for it was off this reef on the south coast of the island that an American brig with the unassuming name of *Elisa* was wrecked in the year 1808. That event changed the history of Fiji as radically as the Norman Conquest changed the history of England.

In the annals of the Fijis, the *Elisa* is reckoned a ship of evil omen. She brought in her trail massacre by muskets of a people who could retaliate only with hand-thrown spears and clubs. Such was the fate also of the Saxons who faced with axes the bows of the Norman invaders. But out of the wreck of the *Elisa* came the rise to power of one tiny tribe on the island of Mbau which eventually united the whole group, making Fiji into one nation instead of a hodgepodge of warring tribes and villages.

The *Elisa* before reaching the Fijis had stopped at Tongatabu having cleared from Port Jackson in Australia. She carried a curious cargo—a quantity of firearms and some forty thousand Spanish dollars. At Tongatabu two gaunt white men, their clothing in ribbons came out to the ship in a canoe and begged to be taken aboard as members of the *Elisa*'s crew. They gave their names as John Husk and Charles Savage and they said they were part of the crew of the

47

British privateer *Port au Prince* which had rounded Cape Horn after raiding Spanish ships off South America and had come to Tonga where the ship had been attacked and most of the crew killed.

There had been such a ship which had been raided by the Tongans for its guns and supplies and the men's story was accepted though not necessarily believed.

Of the two men Savage was the more intelligent and outspoken. He was tall, muscular, fair haired, and quick of mind. He spoke Tongan fluently and Fijian to a limited degree, for the Fijians were at the time in touch with the Tongans and had considerable influence among them.

Captain Cory of the *Elisa* signed the men on, glad to have in his crew someone who could converse with the Fijians for he was bound for these islands. He set his course for Sandalwood Bay on Vanua Levu but his navigation was faulty and toward dusk, with a brisk wind blowing, the *Elisa* piled up on the Mothea Reef off Nairai.

The reef is as bad as there is in the Fijis. It lies nine miles south of the island of Nairai with six hundred feet of water on the seaward side. Its lip just breaks the surface. From the sea the reef can scarcely be seen for the surf breaking over the top shows only toward the shore. The *Elisa* drove down on the reef in the dark, crashed into it with all sails set, and was wrecked in a moment. Fortunately, though there was a brisk wind blowing, the ocean was calm and the crew was able to get into the ship's longboat and go ashore. They took with them thirty-four thousand dollars, navigating instruments, muskets, a cask of powder and ball and cutlasses. They made the journey to the shore safely and set about burying the dollars on the orders of the captain. They were not long ashore, however, before the natives appeared.

Captain Cory had to make a decision whether to fight or make friends. Savage advised him not to fight and spoke to the Fijians in their own tongue. They were delighted to find among the white men, who were the first to land on their island, one who could talk to them.

They put aside their clubs and spears and treated the castaways with kindness. But they stripped them of all their clothes and took away their guns and swords, not out of hostility but because these things were great wonders to them. They also confiscated a number of the dollars which had not yet been buried but they put no value on them, knowing nothing of money.

Savage now emerged as the head man of the castaways because of his knowledge of the Fijian language. He had a powerful personality and great courage which was something the Fijians have always admired. A warrior waved a club at him but Savage did not flinch but stood quite steady and went on with whatever conversation he was engaged in. The Fijians admired this and looked to Savage as the chief of the white men.

In a few days Savage had such influence with the islanders that he persuaded the local chieftain to allow Captain Cory and four others to leave in the longboat for Sandalwood Bay, taking with him six thousand dollars. Others of the crew were also allowed to leave. But Savage did not go. He had discovered that the Fijians knew nothing of muskets. He found himself for the first time in his wretched sailor's life a person of importance, served with *kava* immediately after the chief and allowed to make free with the women of the island who were honored by his advances.

A plan began to take shape in his mind—a plan in which, with the use of a musket, he would make himself a king and live a life such as few men had ever dreamed of.

Savage managed to get hold of one of the muskets from the wreck of the *Elisa* and gave a demonstration of his skill. He was a natural rifleman and never missed his target and soon his fame was such that chieftains were coming from

49

neighboring islands to see him fire his musket. It was a tremendous wonder to them.

The crew of a canoe from the island of Mbau on the southeast tip of Viti Levu arrived and was so impressed it begged the chieftain of Nairai to let Savage return with them to Mbau to be "the white man of the *vanivulu*." The *vanivulu* means "the root of war" and is the title of the chiefs of Mbau. Tui Lawaki, the chief of Nairai, was persuaded to part with Savage. Perhaps he saw in him a threat to his own authority.

Savage went to Mbau to become a member of the court of Naulivou, the chieftain there, and Naulivou soon put him to use. Mbau at the time was an insignificant place, threatened by many enemies, particularly a tribe at the village of Kasavu on the Rewa River on the main island of Viti Levu. Naulivou wanted to attack the village and Savage said he would guarantee him the victory. Whether he had a musket and shot with him or not is not known. According to one story he hadn't, but he found an old musket hanging outside a *bure* or house and repaired it and found enough powder and shot for his purposes.

He was now ready to give a demonstration of the power of his super-weapon. The attackers went up the Rewa River in canoes. The village stood on the banks of the river and was surrounded by a war fence of reeds which was proof against spear and club but not against musket shot.

Savage halted his canoe in the middle of the river a hundred yards from the war fence and opened fire. Every ball brought down a victim. Soon the dead were so numerous that the defenders piled their bodies up to protect them from the terrible weapon of the white man. An ooze of blood trickled from under the war fence to stain the water of the river and the villagers finally surrendered. Not a club or a spear reached Savage in his canoe and single-handed he won the war for his new master. He had done more than win the battle how-

50

ever. He had spread fear among the people—fear of Mbau. Mbau's rise to power dated from this moment.

Another ancient enemy of the people of Mbau were those of Verata, a much more powerful tribe who claimed dominance over Mbau. The chief of Mbau had many times attacked Verata and had each time been beaten. Savage undertook to reverse the picture. Alone he defeated the warriors of Verata who were appalled at seeing men fall dead at the will of a white man a long way off who pointed a stick at them. On this occasion, Savage did not have matters all his own way. Though he won the battle almost single-handed, he was himself wounded. But he continued to fight despite his wounds and this increased his prestige in the eyes of the Fijians.

With Verata defeated he turned on the people of Nakelo where he improved his technique. He had a platform erected so he could shoot over the top of the war fence around the village. Again the defenders were astonished at seeing their companions fall and they took the discharge of the musket for thunder. The story went around and for a long time was believed that Savage, raising his arms to the level of his shoulder and holding a stick in a certain fashion, could summon the gods to his aid and kill any who dared defy him.

Savage, in these one-man massacres, showed loyalty to his own kind. When he attacked Verata he heard that there were four white men in the village. He sent them a secret warning to get out before he started his slaughter. He would not permit cannibalism in his presence. The men who fell to his musket and which represented war booty and excellent food were not to be eaten, and on several occasions he shot in cold blood Fijians whom he came across feasting on human flesh. Because of the terror and awe in which he was held he was able to quell for a while the practice of cannibalism, at least while he was around.

The power of Mbau, an insignificant people, increased fast

because of the work of Savage and his musket. His plans for becoming the greatest man in Fiji bore fruit and he had soon built up a company of musketeers formed of other whites on the island, some of them survivors of the wreck of the *Elisa*.

He was able to keep muskets in the hands of the whites alone for a while, through a stratagem. He encouraged the belief that only white men could handle the weapon and reinforced this belief by a simple demonstration. He gave a musket overcharged with powder to a warrior to fire, telling him to aim at a particular target. The musket, when discharged, kicked so violently that it knocked the man to the ground and broke his jawbone. The target was unscathed and the lesson to be drawn from this was that the new weapon could be controlled only by white men and, used by Fijians, turned against them in anger and injured them.

Probably another reason why the musket remained a white man's weapon for a long time in Fiji was that the few given to the natives were lacking parts and so would not fire, or their barrels were so weak that they burst on being discharged. Muskets with barrels bent slightly out of true were given to the natives as great gifts after awhile but they could not hit what they aimed at and so the belief remained that only the white man knew the secret of the killing thunder.

All the whites in Savage's band were united in denouncing cannibalism. However brutal their own backgrounds (and some of them were criminals convicted of the most atrocious crimes), they would not countenance either cannibalism or the strangling of widows. Sometimes they fought over these matters and sometimes they tried to buy the life of a condemned woman out of mercy—a strange quality in men who would shoot down their defenseless fellows with impunity. They lived a life of the grossest license and often, drunk on trade gin, quarreled with each other, killed each other, or killed natives who looked on them as friends. Over these killings they had not a stir of conscience. On one occasion a white castaway fell into disfavor with a chief who placed a tabu on him forbidding anyone to give the man food. The other whites let him starve to death though he begged them miserably for scraps to eat.

The reward that Savage and all his men sought for their slaughtering services was women. In their own lands women, except the professionals of the waterfront, were beyond their reach. In Fiji they were plentifully available and all of them had a dozen or more wives and displayed the morality of the barnyard, swapping wives with each other and taking any woman who stirred them for the moment. They became more ruthless and more cruel, and more lecherous than the natives and after awhile the awe in which they were first held turned to disgust.

When they fought among themselves the Fijian men rejoiced and they were soon helping in the killing of white men. One Fijian chief in later years, dealing with one of these riffraff, placed him under a irksome tabu. The beachcomber approached a missionary and asked him to use his influence to have the tabu removed. He had committed some offense and then lied about it, blaming another. The missionary got the truth of the matter out of the man and then went to the chief to intercede. The chief, a pagan, listened to the story and pronounced his judgment.

"This man is worthless," he said. "He has tried to blame another for his offenses. Since you plead for him, I will remove the tabu. But tell him that a stranger is welcome everywhere in Fiji but a liar is an enemy to all men."

Savage, though callous when it came to killing in battle, was not as depraved as the greater part of the other whites. He had numerous wives, many of them highly placed in the society of Fiji, rather than among the common women of the village. The Fijians were the only people of the South Seas who accorded respect to others than chieftains.

53

They were cannibals who could say "please" and "thank you" in their own tongue, and who had in their language the equivalent of "sir" and "madam." A warrior who had clubbed another man to death was given a new name with the title *koroi* attached which one might think of as the European equivalent of knighthood in the days of chivalry. But men were honored also for nobility of character, for generosity and for keeping their word; and the Fijian, meeting a stranger, always addressed him as "sir" as a mark of respect.

Savage earned the respect of the chiefs and they gave him their daughters in marriage because of this. He, himself, observed their customs carefully and learned to speak many of their dialects. He had many children but no sons which caused him pain. Later he discovered the reason. If a male child were born to him the mother or the midwife strangled it on order. The chieftains did not want a new line of claimants to their power to arise based on descent from Lord Savage. The grim penalty Savage paid for the power obtained by the slaughter of his musket was the murder of all his sons.

For five splendid years Savage lived in Mbau and like the Normans in England in the eleventh century built a dynasty by raising the power of Mbau which was to change the whole course of Fijian history. Tribe after tribe became tributaries of Mbau and Savage was given the title of Koroi-na Vunivalu, which can be roughly translated as "Man Slayer of the Root of War."

In May of 1813, Savage took some men to go to the Sandalwood Coast on Vanua Levu to help the captain of the ship *Hunter* to get sandalwood. The captain had had a quarrel with the natives of the village of Wailea about sixty miles up the coast and had destroyed some of their canoes. He wished to beach his cutter for repairs but feared that while it was on the beach the Wailea people would attack. To prevent this, he persuaded Savage to attack the village.

A reinforcement arrived in September from Mbau and Sav-

54

age marched inland against the village. He burned the houses, and when he was about to withdraw his forces, found himself cut off by an ambush. A hot battle took place and Savage, Peter Dillon, who was one of the *Hunter*'s men, and seven others including curiously, a Chinaman and two of the Mbau chiefs, hacked their way to an eminence called Black Rock which lay near the shore.

When they got to the rock they saw their allies from Mbau sailing away in their canoes and so were left to face alone a hundred or more infuriated warriors. These dared not storm the rock and face Savage's musket and so there was an impasse which lasted for several hours. At the end of that time Savage grew impatient and left the rock to negotiate a peace.

He spotted among the Waileans some warriors he knew and, putting his trust in their friendship and the awe in which he was held, walked through the others to talk to them. He might have succeeded except that the Chinaman decided to leave the rock and join Savage. The Chinaman was immediately clubbed and then the spell that protected Savage was broken. He was seized, up-ended, and his head held down in a pool of water until he was drowned. His body was immediately cut up, together with that of the Chinaman, before the eyes of his companions on the rock, and put into an oven to be cooked.

Robson, captain of the *Hunter*, sent eight hostages he had aboard in return for the lives of the rest of the men. One of the priests of Wailea ascended the rock to assure the men there that they could go to the boat and would not be hurt. Dillon, however, did not trust the priest and seized him and marched him with a musket in his back through the crowd until he and the rest were able to escape.

That was the end, then, of Charles Savage, who introduced the musket into the wars of Fiji making future wars far more terrible than those of the past and laying the foundation for

55

the rise to dominance of the chiefs of Mbau. He was drowned, cooked and eaten. And yet, unwittingly, his executioners paid a tribute to the seaman who for five years had been a king.

They split the bones of his arms and thighs and made needles out of them—sail needles.

Chapter Eight

THERE is to this day unlifted treasure on the island of Nairai. It consists of many thousands of silver dollars buried by Captain Cory and his men after the wreck of the *Elisa*—as yet uncovered. These are Spanish dollars of the late eighteenth century which at that time were the international unit of currency and indeed so well known in the United States that Thomas Jefferson in 1782 recommended that the dollar become the basic American coin. These dollars, then, are worth far more than their face value.

There were forty thousand of them on the *Elisa* and thirty-four thousand were taken off in the longboat. Of these, six thousand were taken away when Captain Cory left the island of Nairai. A further nine thousand dollars were recovered from the natives who traded them for trinkets, not knowing their value. This would leave about nineteen thousand dollars still unaccounted for and there have been many treasure hunts for the horde without success.

Occasionally one of the dollars turns up. There is a Fijian game which is played by skidding a long stick with a weight at one end on the ground. One visitor to Nairai found children playing this game using for the weight some of the old Spanish dollars off the *Elisa*.

Rob recently dived off the Mothea Reef on which the *Elisa* was wrecked and found a few pieces of the ship's timbers in the coral which he presented to the museum at Suva. But although about six thousand dollars went down with the ship there is no likelihood of these being recovered for silver soon deteriorates to a black powder in salt water.

Like many of the islands of the Fijis, Nairai is difficult to get to. There is as yet no organized transportation to many of the remoter islands of the group. To reach them one has to wait for a copra boat and bargain with the skipper for passage. I wanted to go to Nairai and the journey consumed a week although the distance from Viti Levu is less than two hundred miles.

I left Suva in a bus that bucketed along a dirt road to a little village some miles out of the principal city. The road plunged up a flank of hills and down the valleys, turning and twisting like a roller coaster. The driver, an East Indian, added to the zest of the journey by trying to race a bus ahead of him. Since there certainly did not seem to be room for him to pass, should he overtake the other, there appeared to be little point in the race. However, to my horror he did overtake the bus ahead and did pass him with two wheels on the road and two in the jungle to the side. There was no extra charge for this performance.

At the village I got out with my fellow passengers who were all Fijians visiting the island of Ovalau for which we were bound as the first stage of the journey to Nairai. Rob had told me that from Ovalau I could get a copra boat which would take me to the island. He did not know when the copra boat would leave and indeed it was impossible for it to run on a schedule, the boat being entirely at the mercy of the wind.

I wanted to go to Nairai because it was the place of the *Elisa*'s wreck and for another reason as well. This was my second trip to the Fiji Islands. I had returned to gather material about them for this book, taking a plane and landing at Nandi Airport in the northwest corner of Viti Levu. I stayed at the New Macombo Hotel and met an old friend, Marie Hardwick, whom I had first met at the Grand Pacific in Suva where she was the manager. I told her my purpose in returning to Fiji and when I had gone to my room a Fijian girl knocked at the door and came in to tidy up. She seemed to take a long time about it and at last said, "Sir, I hear you want to visit the other islands."

I replied that I did. I was sitting in a chair and she sat on the floor at my feet like a child looking up at me.

"I hope you will go to my island—Nairai," she said. "Everybody there would be happy to see you. They would all make you welcome." She hesitated and added, "I hope you will go, sir, and if you do, tell the *buli* that I am well and his brother is well also."

"You know the *buli?*" I asked.

"Oh, yes. He is my brother-in-law."

"What is your name?"

"I am Eleanor Gaunavou," she replied.

So I had to go to Nairai to tell the *buli* that his sister-in-law and his brother, working in the hotel far away in Nandi, were both well.

The launch that took me to Ovalau carried perhaps a hundred passengers in seats as on a double-decker bus. Among them was a young Englishman from the city of Leeds in Yorkshire. For baggage he had only a knapsack. His profession was that of a school teacher and tiring of the raw climate of Yorkshire he had set out for the South Seas almost without money beyond his fare. He was earning his living by teaching in schools in British territory throughout the South Pacific. He had been three years away from home, was as poor as ever, but enormously rich in experience. He sought the out-of-the-way places and thought nothing of sleeping on the beach or in the jungle undergrowth in a sleeping bag if no better bed offered.

Ovalau has only one town, notorious in the old days of whaling and blackbirding. The name of the town is Levuka and it is to all intents and purposes but one street wide. The main street is all it has and that flanks the bay with houses only on the landward side. A hundred years ago every third building in Levuka was a grog shop selling squareface trade gin and it was said that ships approaching the island could find their way by the empty gin bottles floating in the ocean.

Levuka still has about it a wild look. A great tumble of hills rises behind the town as if to shovel the clapboard buildings into the bay. The bay itself is fringed with a terrible reef with only one passage marked by a light which must surely be invisible at night against the lights of the town. You shoot in through the reef passage from the wild exterior water into the green lagoon, and hold your breath as you see the towers of coral reaching up from the bottom.

There is one hotel in Levuka run by one of the great characters of Fiji, Ed Ashley. He is a big man full of tales and always ready to talk and for a week, while waiting for a copra boat, I talked with Ed who fed me beer and sandwiches and wild tales of the past of Fiji. The name of the hotel is the Royal and it may be one of the oldest buildings in the Fijis. It is stoutly built, beyond a doubt, but the floors are all uneven and there is a tangle of flowering vines running up the facade, wild and luxurious and entirely enchanting. There are two stories and a balcony runs around the second story so you can walk from your bedroom onto the balcony in your dressing gown, flop into a deck chair, which has extentions on the arms on which to rest your feet, and drink your morning tea while watching the wild reef and delighting in the piratical atmosphere of the town.

Levuka is the last harbor of the old characters of the South Seas and it was properly at Levuka that I met my only pirate. He was a big Fijian who lumbered up one day as I sat waiting for news of a copra boat and introduced himself to me, accepting a cup of tea though I discovered later he much preferred beer.

"My name, sir," he said, "is Nadriubalavu."

60

"Has it a meaning?" I asked, delighted at such a name.

"Yes," he replied. "It means the Light That Can Be Seen From Afar. I am of the chiefly people."

We chatted about this and that and he begged me to come to his village which lay a little to the west of Levuka and was noted for the fact that there was a fountain in it in the form of a lion with water spouting from its mouth. This, he assured me, was a great wonder. Since I was not interested in stone lions but only in copra boats, I declined the invitation. We warmed to each other, however, and he confessed that he worked in Viti Levu selling insurance, that he had returned to Ovalau for a holiday and he was waiting for some money to be sent to him which was owed as commission on the policies he had sold.

"It is tiresome going to the post office waiting for money," he said, and I nodded, for in my travels I have many times been through that experience and it is tiresome indeed.

"Would you, sir, do me a favor?" he asked.

"Gladly, if it is in my power," I replied.

"My vacation is being spoiled by this waiting for money," said the Light That Can Be Seen From Afar. "You are returning to Suva. Could you lend me a little money and I will give you a letter to the manager of the insurance company in Suva for whom I work and he will repay you."

"How much money do you need?" I asked.

"Twenty pounds," he replied.

I gave him ten being overtaken by an unaccustomed caution. He pocketed the check in a chiefly manner and I did not see him again. When I returned to Suva I discovered that the insurance company knew nothing of him and so I lost my ten pounds.

But in view of the fact that my ancestors or people representing my ancestors had sold to his ancestors chunks of elephant tusks in the pretense that they were whales' teeth to obtain precious sandalwood, I think he was entitled to level the score.

At Levuka also I met Robin, a big, gentle, slow-spoken man who worked in or ran (I was not sure which) a machine shop near to the hotel. We talked of wrecks and I told him of a large yawl I had had a hand in raising when it sunk off the California coast. We used inner tubes which we filled with air on the bottom and, having attached them to the hull first, the yawl came up readily with the one hundredth and fortieth tube. Robin was not impressed. He had helped to raise a boat which had gone down in a storm off Ovalau in a hundred feet of water.

"You could see her on the bottom," said Robin, his eyes wide with wonder like a child's. "There were fish swimming over her and you could make out the top of the deckhouse and some of the deck and I thought I would like to bring her up. But I would have to get divers and there weren't any diving suits about. And if there were, there wasn't a compressor and if there was a compressor, I don't know who I could have got to run it. So I had to get men who could hold their breath and go down a hundred feet and tie a bowline on a big pad eye that was amidships on the vessel. With that tied, I could haul her up for there was air trapped in her and she wouldn't be so heavy.

"Two men said they would do the diving for me. They said that they had been down a hundred feet many times and it would be nothing to tie the bowline to the pad eye. Well, the first put on his goggles and got hold of the hawser in one hand and a big stone in the other and jumped in and down he went.

"I looked over the side at him and I could see that he was in trouble so I pulled him up again and he was bleeding from the eyes and nose and ears, and I thought that was the end of that and the boat would have to lie on the bottom.

"But the other fellow said he could do it and though I

didn't want to let him try, he said there would be nothing to it and the only reason his friend was bleeding was because he had had a bit of a night of it the evening before. So down he went with the cable and he was down so long I thought he'd drowned but he came up again and he'd not only tied the towline for me but brought the sextant that was down in the cabin. And that's the truth as I am standing here talking to you."

I believed Robin for some of the island divers can go down to astonishing depths and do so to get valuable shells. Of these, the golden cowrie is the most valuable that has come out of Fiji so far and the market price, when I was there, was around sixty dollars each.

While I waited for the copra boat that didn't come, I picked up stories of Levuka and odd little bits of information about the old wild days of the island. Squareface gin, for instance. I knew it was called squareface because it came in square bottles but why square bottles? The answer is that you can pack more square bottles than round bottles into a case and every bottle imported provided a nice profit for the grog shops.

East of Levuka, lying forlorn upon the shore, is a famous modern Fijian wreck. It is the wreck of the *Joyita*, a mystery ship which continued the ghostly tradition of the famous *Marie Celeste*. The *Marie Celeste*, a schooner, was found at sea in perfect condition under sail but without a soul on board and no trace of her passengers or crew or what happened to them was ever discovered.

So it was with the *Joyita*. She sailed from Suva with twenty or so people aboard, disappeared and was found floating close to Ovalau and utterly deserted. There was, however, a clue to the reason why she had been abandoned. She was half full of water and listing badly. An examination showed that the exhaust hose, through which the water for cooling the engine was pumped overboard, had burst. For some time the

63

engine had been sucking in ocean water and pumping it into the bottom of the boat. By the time the captain discovered this, his bilge pump was submerged and wouldn't work. He had seemingly tried to rig a drive for the bilge pump off the main engine but the water had risen so fast that the main engine quit.

There still remained the mystery of why everybody had left the boat for it was well known that unless she broke up she was unsinkable. All the spare spaces in her hull were crammed with cork. Perhaps there was an outbreak of panic and the passengers left the ship in the boats and compelled the captain to go with them. But whatever became of them is a mystery and is likely to remain one. Not a trace of them ¡was found.

I think I was in Levuka for a week and on the way to becoming an island character myself when one evening a man called at the Royal Hotel and announced that he was the captain of the copra boat and he would be sailing for Nairai in a couple of hours.

He was not a Fijian but a tall, light-skinned and pleasant-faced East Indian. His name was Faiz Khan. I thanked him, dashed up to my room, packed my bag, and hurried downtown with it to board the copra boat. It lay alongside the wharf and I had to step down to get into it.

The cabin covered the whole deck. I handed down my suitcase and typewriter through a small door in the side of the cabin and crawled in myself. An oil lamp hung from a deck timber and by its light I could see a number of Fiji women full of smiles and merriment carrying unknown goods in plaited baskets and sitting in the hold of the ship.

The ship was all hold, and the engine, a three-cylinder English Lister diesel, lay in plain view amidships. Captain Khan showed me a board bunk in the forward part of the hold and said it was for my use. It was, I believe, the only bunk aboard and properly belonged to him. The copra boat was no more than twenty-five feet long with a beam of perhaps nine feet. The steersman stood on a little platform in the middle of the hold with his head and shoulders above the top of the cabin so that all that was visible of him was his trunk and legs.

While he was steering he handled the engine controls with his feet and looked rather like an organist who plays one set of keys with his hands and, doing a kind of dance upon his bench, plays another set of monstrous keys below him with his feet. I had tried while at Levuka to find out how far away Nairai was. But in the Fijis distance is not regarded and to this question I could get no firm answer. Indeed, although I made the journey myself in Captain Khan's copra boat, I cannot say how far Nairai lies from Ovalau.

It is a long way, though.

Chapter Nine

IT was dark when we left Levuka and just before we sailed a stiff sea wind swept in from the Koro Sea and set up a short chop in the water in the lagoon behind the reef. There was no sense in my remaining on deck which consisted, in any case, of the top of the cabin which extended the full width of the copra boat. So I stayed below, sitting with bent shoulders for lack of room on the plank bunk, trying to pick up a word or two of the talk of the plump and pleasant-looking Fiji women all dressed in flowered cotton frocks as if there was but one source of clothing for all of them—a source that provided only one pattern.

The women of Fiji have a distinctive and attractive dress. They wear a flowered outer frock which comes somewhat below the knee. Under this they wear a long petticoat down to the ankles so that a foot or more of it shows below the hem of the frock. The petticoat is of thin silky material. The dress I was told derived from the missionaries. The petticoat was originally a *sulu* or wrap-around garment which, when worn at all, was worn high over the breasts leaving the lower parts exposed.

The missionaries prevailed on the Fijians, who were very good-natured in this matter, to lower the *sulu* which of course covered the lower parts but left the breasts exposed. The solution was to put on another garment which would cover the breasts and out of this arrangement came the modern dress of the Fijian women. At least that was the story that was given me.

66

Although I was down below I knew immediately when we went out through the passage of the reef. The copra boat seemed to hesitate for a moment as if catching its breath. Then, its head lifted and the stern went down and there was a shriek from the women in which laughter was mingled with fear and they all fell jouncing against each other. I was nearly thrown out of my bunk on top of them. We had met the first of the rollers of the Koro Sea.

From then on the weather grew increasingly wild. We clawed into wind and sea with sails set and the diesel pounding away to help. The smell of copra—warm, excessively oily, and somewhat musty—was mixed with hot fumes from the diesel engine. The boat reared and lurched and at times seemed to drop several feet as if it had fallen from the top of a cliff. The descent was so fast on such occasions that my stomach rose in that nervous reaction one gets when going down in a very fast elevator.

All about was the wild slosh and crash of the water and above this a little sibilance or whistling of wind. The sole lantern we had for illumination, protected in a cage of wire, swung and danced on the ceiling beam and by its light I could see the lower torso and legs of the helmsman. It is rather curious, I thought to myself, to put one's life in the care of half a human being for that was all I could see of him. The legs were thin but muscular and the right foot seemed to have the job of operating the accelerator. When we met a big roller, the foot, with agility, reached into the gloom and pushed the accelerator lever forward to give us the needed power to climb the side of the roller. The top reached, the foot quickly pulled the accelerator back to slow us as we went down the other side lest we plunge our bow into the ocean.

We did that several times, indeed a score of times, when the seas were too steep, or the foot, groping in the gloom, missed its mark. The copra boat would shudder and vibrate and the effect on the passengers was that of sitting inside a large drum which someone was pounding with a wet pillow. The boat would seem to stop altogether for a moment, there would be a wild rush of water over the top and then a tremendous vibration as the propeller came completely out of the sea astern and whirled in the air. Then the little copra boat would recover its grip, raise its sturdy bow and prepare for the next onslaught of the sea.

The whole trade of the Fijis depends on these little copra boats which are built by amateurs without reference to any design or plan. They carry passengers and mail from island to island, pick up fifty or a hundred sacks of copra, the output and total substance of tiny plantations and carry it to market. These copra boats represent a sturdy, cocky, beggar's fleet of merchant ships to which no tribute is ever made but upon which the economy of the scattered islands depends. I doubt that any of their captains could secure papers from the Coast Guard or the Board of Trade certifying to their knowledge of navigation and seamanship. I am quite sure that none of the boats would pass a United States Coast Guard inspection as to their seaworthiness and ability to carry freight and passengers. Yet they are out in all weather, and their captains can handle them with a skill and courage that shows the highest seamanship. They know nothing of sextants and chronometers, carry no charts, have never heard of a rhumb line, yet they go from island to island as freely and as certainly as birds. There are disasters, however. Shortly after my own voyage, a copra boat back from Nairai overturned in a gust of wind and all aboard, except one woman, were drowned.

When daylight came and I was able to gain the deck—by crawling out of the side of the cabin over the water and hauling myself up—I looked at the boat's mast and rigging and marveled. The mast was a slender, untrimmed trunk of a young tree. It was unpainted, unvarnished and had several splits running up it. The stays supporting the mast were rusty wire which, clean, might serve for a clothesline. All, in short, was no better rigged than Huckleberry Finn's raft. And yet it served and served well.

I got little sleep that night. I am fortunate in that I am not readily made seasick, otherwise the combination of fumes from the diesel engine, the copra and the pitching of the boat would have been my undoing. But several times I was tossed bodily upward from my bunk against the cabin top overhead and finally I was compelled to get what rest I could lying on the bunk with one hand stretched upward to brace me against the ceiling.

The worst of the weather came in the small hours of the morning. The mainsail split and had to be taken down. Without its aid in steadying the boat, she pitched and rolled abominably. The women gathered in a dismal little clump, holding each other for comfort and praying. I wondered vaguely about life jackets and lifeboats and sharks and with these uncomfortable thoughts fell asleep again.

When I woke in the morning the sea was still rough but the wind had moderated. I poked my head out over the water and saw a scowling sky with black clouds so low that they seemed in the distance to be brushing the top of the sea. The sea was not the azure tropical sea at which I had been looking but the scowling green-gray winter sea of Europe.

One of the crew brought me breakfast. I got a fine big mug of hot tea with sweet condensed milk in it and some large hard biscuits covered with salty butter. Maybe they were ship's biscuits, but I enjoyed them although much of the tea, due to the motion of the boat, fell into my lap. It warmed my thighs for awhile and I was glad of that for they were cold.

We stopped at a little island which I took for Nairai but it was Matiki, about halfway to our destination. Then we went on again, having off-loaded some merchandise, much of it bound up in used brown paper and used string and toward afternoon came at last to Nairai. The copra boat anchored just outside the reef and amid gusts of wind and squalls of rain we climbed into a little boat to be taken ashore.

My immediate problem of course was to find somewhere to stay. I had Eleanor's introduction to her brother-in-law, the *buli*, but he was not on the island. Captain Khan, of the copra boat, however, had taken everything in hand. It is one of the characteristics of these people that, without any thought of profit, they make your problems theirs. He told me that I was to stay at his house and would hear of no other solution.

He took my gear himself and came in the boat with me to see me safely ashore and take me to his house. A shelf of coral as sharp as broken glass extends from the village of Natauloa off which we were anchored about two hundred yards to sea. The beach is of sand; then there is the coral and then a sharp drop-off where the copra boat was anchored.

There is, at low tide, from one to three feet of water over this coral shelf onto which I stepped from the boat. With my trousers rolled up as high as they would go, a typewriter in one hand and a suitcase in the other, I started ashore. I had had some experience with coral and though I had taken off my shoes which were hung by the laces around my neck, kept on my socks which were a great comfort to my feet.

Seeing my predicament Captain Khan took the typewriter, someone else, already heavily laden, took the suitcase and another, bending down, indicated that I was to climb on his back and he would carry me ashore. In defense of my own manliness I rejected this favor, but even with my socks on, my feet were cut and bruised by the time I gained the beach. I was slower than the rest who could walk over coral barefoot carrying heavy burdens without any hurt.

The sea life in the shallow, clear water fascinated me. Writhing, hairy arms of serpent stars groped for food from every crevice. There were several dozen big sea slugs called Bêche-de-Mer lying about and in one little pool a tiny octopus which I reached to pick up for they are the friendliest of creatures and have a surprising intelligence. But he filled the

70

whole of the little basin with sepia ink and I could not find him.

When I arrived on the beach a host of children had come out of the thatched huts of the village to stare solemnly at me. They were neither smiling nor frowning. Their look was one of pure wonder. I was the first white man they had ever seen and so a great marvel to them.

I had had the forethought to buy a few bags of candy and I reached in my pockets and handed some to the children. They came gravely forward, took the candy, stepped gravely back again, took off the paper and popped the candy in their mouths. There was no discussion among them and no giggling. They were as serious as scientists experiencing a new marvel. There was no shyness among them and no forwardness. Indeed, they had all the dignity of Roman senators.

Captain Khan lived in a pretty little bungalow at one end of the village. His was the only house constructed in the European manner, its walls being of wood though its roof was of corrugated iron—the eternal roofing of the tropics if pandanus or coconut thatch is not used. His wife had the same name as the island, Nairai, and she was a Fijian, plump and dark and good natured. She was very concerned for my welfare after my rough voyage and fixed some dinner for us right away. After dinner she got a room of the bungalow ready for me (I suspect it belonged to her eldest son who went to sleep elsewhere), and I lay down for a few minutes but did not wake up until the following morning.

There are in Viti Levu a great number of East Indians who were imported on labor contracts as will be explained later. They live apart from from the Fijians. The two races coexist but scarcely mingle. They do not even worship together for the East Indians tend to cling to the religions of India while the Fijians are all Christian. There is no hostility that I could discern, nor is there any great amity. Intermarriage is rare.

And yet here was Faiz Khan of Indian ancestry married

71

to a woman who was entirely Fijian, and they obviously doted on each other and had numerous children who were as merry as one could wish. He told me he had waited a great number of years to marry his wife, having met her when he came to Nairai to work on a plantation there. The plantation was owned by a Mr. Baker, long dead when I arrived. When his work on the plantation was done, Faiz Khan had to go back to Viti Levu and he stayed there some years before he was able to return and marry his wife.

Mr. Baker, I believe, was the only white man to settle on Nairai. He bought some land and started a plantation of coconuts. The islanders all welcomed and helped him and worked for him voluntarily in the bad years when crops were uncertain and prices appallingly low. Eventually he prospered, as much because of the generosity of the islanders as because of his own hard work and courage. Before he died he decided to give back to the islanders some of the help they had given him. He encouraged them to start little plantations of their own, built jetties from the villages to help with the loading of copra, built schools and houses and left provision in his will for this work to be continued. Shortly before his death he asked Faiz Khan, who had worked for him and was now an independent trader on his own and the owner of a copra boat, to take care of his widow.

"One day I will come to America," Faiz Khan told me, "but I must stay here for the time being to take care of Mrs. Baker while she is alive."

Mrs. Baker, who is in her eighties, lives alone in a lovely home on a hillside among neat gardens full of flowers. She is taken care of in her old age not only by Faiz Khan but by all the islanders who, out of love for her and her husband, rush to do anything she wants. Her house is cleaned, her garden is cared for, her meals are cooked, her laundry is done by the people of Nairai as a work of love. Mr. Baker himself could not take better care of his wife and when the

72

islanders speak of him it is with great affection, as if a saint had lived among them in the form of a coconut planter.

"He was of the chiefly kind," they say and no greater tribute can be rendered in Fiji than that.

I thought to call on Mrs. Baker but feared to disturb her and so did not do so. In any case it was midwinter. The sun, if it shone at all, did so only for a few minutes and the rain lashed down in white squalls so that I was constantly scampering for shelter in my walks about the island, either under coconut palms or into someone's hut.

In one of these walks through the village which consisted of less than two dozen huts, all of thatch, I was invited into the house of a young Fijian, Sakinsa Ulgiviti. He was, he told me, a relative of the *buli* but whether he was a brother or a brother-in-law I could not make out. He spoke very little English and his young wife, who sat on the mat floor near me, spoke no English at all.

The interior of the house contained no furniture. Its floor was covered by a pandanus mat. The household utensils, pots and pans and the bowl for mixing *kava*, were hung on the walls. There was a picture of Queen Elizabeth II and an aging photograph of a splendid Fijian seated in a carved Victorian chair whom I presume was my host's grandfather. We tried to talk, earnestly struggling with the simplest words but communication was impossible. So we just sat there in a silent friendship, smoking cigarettes until a tiny cry came from the end of the hut, which was curtained off. The woman went behind the curtains for a moment and then seated herself once more.

"A baby?" I asked. The word is international and the man nodded.

"How old?" I asked.

"Three," said the man.

"Three months?" I asked.

"No. Three days."

73

I turned to the mother and ignoring the fact that she had not a word of English asked if I could see her baby. She was very proud and happy to show the baby to me. It was a tiny, dark morsel swaddled in a pink blanket and lying in a little cot. They would not have shown it to me or mentioned its existance voluntarily, but they were very pleased that I wanted to see it. I very much wanted to pick it up but I didn't dare. It had been born in the hut without any medical care for the mother other than a midwife. And she was already about her work, strong and in excellent health.

It was plain that neither father nor mother was well to do and indeed the whole village was, in our terms, poor. Old pots and kettles were family treasures and cans, with we in America throw away, were kept as useful articles by the villagers. There was one tiny store in the village which sold rice and flour, salt and cloth and cigarettes. I wanted to buy a dozen packets of cigarettes, for in leaving Ovalau I had come without any. But to have done so would have seriously depleted the stock so I contented myself with two.

Cigarettes, I found, are the only things you can give to adult Fijians in return for the many services they offer without pay. Some are so short of them that a cigarette will be shared among two or three. The Fijians never asked me for a cigarette for they all have a natural dignity which would forbid this minor begging. When they accept a cigarette from you it is always with a nod of the head and the word *vinaka* which we translate as "thank you," but is actually the far more satisfactory word "good."

At the end of the village I discovered in one of my walks between rainstorms, a cemetery. A few pebbles laid out in a design marked the graves. There were no headstones and no histories of the deceased. The graves are all within the sound of the surf and there is at all times the sibilance of the trade winds riffling the palm fronds overhead.

The dead of Nairai rest, indeed, in deep peace.

74

Chapter Ten

RAIN pelted down the greater part of the time that I was in Nairai and although it was not cold this rain made traveling about the island very uncomfortable. In Captain Khan's house there was no shower-bath and I wanted very much to have a good scrub and get rid of the smell of copra that seemed to have penetrated my skin. He had a shower in a coconut grove to the rear of the house. It consisted of a chest-high corrugated iron stall with a stand pipe overhead. Here I bathed in a lashing rainstorm and I think more water fell on me from the sky than out of the standpipe. This soft rain water was delightful for bathing, and my bar of soap produced an abundance of suds so I was twice as long rinsing off as I was soaping myself. When I was done the copra smell had gone and for that I was thankful. I don't think I have ever had a more enjoyable shower.

There is no road around Nairai. There are no vehicles on the island, not even a bicycle. I wanted to go around it and so Faiz Khan told me one day that his copra boat was to circle the island picking up a cargo to be taken to Ovalau and I could go with it if I wished. I was glad of the opportunity and went, though I came near to being shipwrecked.

We sailed inside the barrier reef, stopping wherever there was a hut or two huts ashore to pick up copra. Sometimes there was only a sack of copra and sometimes two or three. But at one place there were so many that they constituted a load and a half for the little dinghy that was used to carry the sacks out to the copra boat. The solution of the problem obviously was to make two trips but that was not the solution adopted. The overload of copra was dumped in the dinghy until the sacks were piled so high that the seats disappeared and there was no place to sit down and row.

There was scarcely an inch between the top of the dinghy's sides and the water. The crewman climbed on top of the mountain of copra bags and laughing with glee poled the overloaded dinghy over the coral out to the copra boat, the water lapping in all the time to his delight. The dinghy, touching the side of the copra boat, shipped water so fast that it began to founder. The boatman still chuckling with glee started to fling hundred-pound bags of copra onto the deck to lighten the boat. I have never seen so fast an unloading and the dinghy was saved.

Captain Khan was not with us on this trip, the boat being handled by his Fijian mate, who could not speak English. He had been instructed not to fail to show me where the *Elisa* had been wrecked and when we came to this point at the south of the island, he pointed to the reef and said, "Lisa." A wilder spot would be hard to imagine. There was not much wind but the ocean boiled over the reef in savage white slashes like bared fangs. There was a tiny islet—no more than a rock with a crabbed growth on top of it—and it was on this I understand that the crew of the *Elisa* was picked up.

Shoreward was a bold promontory and the mate, pointing to this, said, "Dollars." This was the only mention of the *Elisa*'s treasure made to me on the island. I do not think the islanders themselves believe there is any money still buried there. Innumerable searches have been made without turning up the hoard. Yet I believe I know where the treasure may be, and I will one day return to look for it.

The circle of the island in the copra boat took all day. I went ashore once or twice to look around and found little plantations of coconut and casava. Children stared at me wherever I landed and when I took pictures of them, they broke into tears and ran fleeing to their parents.

It was dusk when we picked up our last load of copra and we had taken so many sacks aboard that the copra boat lay low in the water. To return to our own village we had now to go a little way beyond the reef for at this point the reef plunged in toward the shore, and the lagoon behind it was too shallow for the boat to pass.

We got under way and headed out toward the reef and when we were still a quarter of a mile from it the sun disappeared and we were plunged into the sudden tropical night. The mate went forward to the bow and signaling with his hand directed the helmsman to the right or left to tread our way through the coral. There were times when he came close to panic and swung around to face the helmsman, gesticulating and shouting to him to put the engine in reverse.

I joined him at the bow in an attempt to spot the coral but could see nothing but black, boding water. The mate, however, had x-ray eyes and brought us through though we touched twice with a grating sound.

We had to clear an outcropping of rock at the seaward end of the reef and, clear of it, swing hard to the right to follow a narrow channel through the coral. We cleared the rock, swung to the right, headed out to sea, and then the steersman shouted something. The mate went flying back to him, the engine was stopped and I discovered that the steering gear had broken down.

The copra boat was steered by a chain that went around the axle of the wheel and around another drum on the rudder itself. It was this chain which had broken. Nobody had to tell me what to expect now. I had flicked a cigarette butt into the water earlier and noted that it drifted fast toward the reef. Without steerage the copra boat would be taken by the current up on the coral and wrecked, and this is what I confidently expected would happen.

There was no sea running and I judged the distance to the shore to be about a mile. The copra boat's dinghy, which, in case of a wreck, would have been available, had been left at the last village so we would have to swim for it. Watching the boat hauled down on the reef by the current, I consoled myself with the thought that the water was a lovely eighty degrees and I could swim in it all night if the sharks would let me.

I am myself not much of a mechanic and certainly do not know how you can repair a broken link in a chain without a cold chisel, an anvil and a heavy hammer. But the mate and his crew of one had no such tools available. They went below and hurling copra sacks aside found the ends of the broken chain.

There was a prolonged silence, broken only by some thumping and I sat on deck watching the white water of the reef come nearer and nearer. There was no sense anchoring. We had about two hundred fathoms under us—much too deep for an anchor. The mate came on deck, took a look at the reef, grinned at me and went below chuckling, for it is a characteristic of the Fijians that they take a boyish delight in danger.

There was some more hammering and now, the moon having come up, I could see the wall of coral rising out of the water no more than a hundred feet from us. I started to take off my shoes and at that moment the engine started up, the mate came on deck and sat down beside me and said, "Fixed."

I gave him a cigarette.

That little episode was a sample of the seamanship of Fijians. One aspect of seamanship, and a very important one, is the ability to fix things without having the necessary tools and materials. A hole in the hull can be fixed by dragging a sail under the hull over the hole. If there is no sail a mattress will serve. If there is no mattress, blankets, foul-weather gear or sacks will serve. Masts can be replaced with booms and if there are no booms, some kind of a mast can be contrived with floorboards. That is seamanship and the Fijians have plenty of it. They had repaired the chain with a long nail which they had pounded with a hammer into a fastening to hold the two links together.

Rob told me, as a demonstration of the seamanship of Fijians, of a man who was fishing in an outrigger off the coast of Viti Levu when a tremendous offshore wind, heralding a hurricane, arose. The wind was of such a velocity that the canoe could not be paddled against it and was blown out to sea. The hurricane lasted for three days and a week after it had died down there was no trace of the man and he was presumed drowned.

His friends prepared a funeral feast for him and as the ceremonies were about to begin he arrived, not by sea, but by bus.

Here was a miracle indeed. He'd been blown off the island by a hurricane and returned on a bus. He explained that when the wind struck he knew he could not make land and that his outrigger would be swamped and there was no sense exhausting himself by bailing. The outrigger, even if full of water, would float provided it was relieved of weight. So he had slipped over the side and remained in the water which now supported his weight for the duration of the hurricane, holding onto the outrigger.

When the wind abated he was hardly strong enough to pull himself aboard, but did so, baled her out, hoisted his little sail, which was in tatters but still serviceable, and made land some thirty miles below his point of departure. There he had borrowed his bus fare and returned to his village.

He did not think a great deal of the feat.

I remained on Nairai for four blustering, rain-swept days, my visit being limited by the need to take Captain Khan's copra boat back. His next trip to Ovalau would have been ten days to two weeks later and though he begged me to stay I could not afford the time. The copra boat sailed at dawn and once more I rolled up my trouser legs and, carrying my typewriter and my suitcase, waded in my socks out to the end of the coral shelf. As I was about to get into the dinghy a figure shouted to me from the beach and a man came wading out carrying a parcel.

He was Sakinsa Ulgiviti, the young Fijian who had entertained me in his hut and the father of the three-day-old baby. He had written his name on the parcel in pencil.

"Not forget," he said giving the parcel to me.

"Not forget," I replied.

We shook hands and I went aboard the copra boat and when we had pulled up the anchor and were headed out to the sea, he stood there on the edge of the coral waving to me that he might not be forgotten. When I opened the parcel it contained two beautiful pandanus sleeping mats of the most expensive kind. He had given me, a stranger, the most valuable possession of his household.

On our way back to Ovalau we had the trade winds behind us. Captain Khan had repaired his sail and the little copra boat, most heavily laden, plunged speedily onward before wind and tide. I didn't mention the broken chain on the steering gear but I hoped it had been better repaired for we met with twelve- and fifteen-foot rollers and put our bow down under them and the strain on the rudder was heavy.

We had been about twenty hours getting to Nairai but got back to Ovalau in eight. Captain Khan would take no money in return for the time I had stayed in his house. He would accept only the fare and took that, I believe, because I had booked through an agent who would want his commission.

When we got into Levuka there was an island steamer at the dock. I hustled ashore and asked where she was bound for and was told Suva. This was a very fortunate chance for otherwise I would have had to remain in Levuka four or five days waiting for the launch to get back to Viti Levu. I sought the captain and asked him whether he could take a passenger. He said he could and I was soon installed in a snug little cabin quite as luxurious as the sundeck of a Cunarder after the little copra boat.

The steamer was taking on a deck cargo of cattle to be slaughtered in Suva. They were half wild and frightened out of their wits but the ship's crew were the best cowpunchers I have ever seen in action. They got a running bowline around the horns, slapped a sling under the belly, and hoisted the kicking, frightened animals aboard in a twinkling. They were tethered on the foredeck so close together that they kicked and gored each other and I felt very sorry for them.

But they had to be transported live and the method of getting them aboard was an improvement on the older system when they were often picked up by their horns or by a leg and swung onto the ship.

The captain and crew of the steamer, with the exception of the first mate, were all Fijians. We left shortly after dusk and arrived off Suva just before dawn. At breakfast, which I had on board, the chief engineer, a Fijian, asked me whether I would like to see a newspaper. Without waiting for a reply he produced a copy of the *Fiji Times* and said, with a big grin, that there was a story on page two that would interest me for it concerned America. I turned to the page and there was the story. The headline read, "RACE RIOT IN CHICAGO—Whites Battle Negroes Over Housing."

I glanced up at the dusky chief engineer and he was still grinning. I felt ashamed. A Fijian had given me, a white stranger, two mats. In our country this same Fijian would be rudely treated as a colored man. The mate's grin was not vicious. It seemed to suggest that we *papalangi* have a lot to learn.

Chapter Eleven

AFTER the death of Savage whose thigh bones may now be unidentified artifacts in the museum in Suva, the real wars in Fiji began. Up to the time of his appearance with his musket the Fijian fighting had resulted in only a few killed in each battle. Now the dead ran into scores.

Following the example of Mbau most of the other chieftains tried to get a few white men with muskets in their armies and these whites, skilled in the use of the weapon, were merciless and treacherous. At one time there were probably a hundred of them on the Sandalwood Coast and the southern coasts of Viti Levu. Ship's captains used them as interpreters and as men who, for a price, would betray the chiefs whose services they had entered. A tidal wave of bloodshed and treachery swept over the Fijis. Chieftains plotted with beachcombers to seize trading vessels for their trade goods and their muskets. Captains of trading vessels plotted with beachcombers to wipe out whole villages in the hope that by so doing they would please a rival chieftain who would then trade with them.

The sandalwood trade was over. The thickets of the precious aromatic wood were cleaned out in ten years and it was now almost impossible to find a single stick of sandalwood in the Fijis.

Sandalwood was replaced by a trade in Bêche-de-Mer. The big sea slug was prized by the Chinese for soup-making. The creatures abounded in the warm Fiji waters and the trade was almost as lush as sandalwood. The slugs are gathered by divers, boiled in salt water for ten minutes, split open and then smoked.

But getting a cargo was a lengthy process and so the captains of trading vessels tried to set up shore factories to prepare cargoes for them ahead of time. This meant having one or more reliable Europeans living ashore in the Fijis. Reliable Europeans were hard to come by. The shore dwellers were still the old beachcombers, some of them men who had mutinied and killed their own ships' officers.

It was an American from New Hampshire who set up the first real shore factory and trading post in the Fijis. His name was David Whippy and he arrived on board a ship commanded by his brother. Being treated very badly on board by the brother who had an impossible set of Puritan rules for building up his character, David jumped ship at Levuka on Ovalau. He was not the usual beachcomber type. The Fijians soon discovered that his word could be relied upon. He did not lie to them and dissuaded them from quarrels out of which no good could come.

He collected a few together and started curing Bêche-de-Mer. He treated the men who worked for him fairly, refused to be drawn into the squabbles of the other beachcombers and had soon gained the complete respect of the Fijians and the complete contempt of the beachcombers.

He learned to speak the Fijian language, took care of the sick and injured and was indeed so different from all the other white men that the Fijians came to realize for the first time that there were good as well as bad people among the whites. It was a surprising discovery, and David Whippy made such an impression on the natives that he was adopted into one of their tribes, an honor which had not been accorded to any of the other whites with the exception of Savage. Shortly after this he was given the position of *Mata-*

ki-vau, that is Ambassador of the chief at Levuka to the chief at Mbau.

This one drop of New England morality and honesty in the person of David Whippy was the first real benefit the Fijians had received from their white invaders. He came not as an outcast lusting for power, liquor and women, but as a Yankee trader and as the trade in Bêche-de-Mer increased there were others who followed him.

For many years theirs was a lost cause.

Mbau had been started on its road to power by Savage and even after his death, the might of Mbau continued to increase. Tribe after tribe became tributary to the chief of the insignificant little island whose warriors, armed with muskets and pikes and under the command of mercenary beachcombers, demanded tribute from as far away as the Lau Islands two hundred miles to the east. The armies of the Fiji kings at this period (for kings they were indeed with court jesters, cup bearers, ambassadors and a cabinet of advisers) looked like a peasant rabble of the French Revolution. Some of the warriors carried muskets which they never learned to fire effectively. Others had slashing cutlasses or bayonets put on the ends of poles to simulate pikes, or carried hatchets like tomahawks. Others still clung to the terrible war clubs and beautifully wrought throwing spears. The muskets had the curious effect of increasing the power of the war club. Discharged at the enemy the fright produced was such that warriors with clubs had only to dash among them and beat in their skulls.

In this time of wars some tribes disappeared altogether. Others disintegrated when their skilled canoe builders and other craftsmen joined the forces of a rival king. And so, following Savage, the number of kingdoms dwindled while those that remained became more and more powerful.

It was tiny Mbau which was destined to bring an end to all this confusion. The insignificant island was originally

84

called Ulu-ni-vuaka, meaning the "Pig's Head." Its inhabitants were, by force of circumstance, sailors and traders, and because the island was so insignificant and weak its rulers had to have a high degree of courage and intelligence to survive.

About the time of the advent of the white man Mbau was ruled by Chief Banuve, a man who, in any country, would have risen to prominence. With a few hundred impoverished islanders as his subjects he started building up his island from the moment he took over the chief's hut.

Completely untrained, he built stone walls in the sea to protect portions of the island from erosion. He built docks of coral for his canoes and he even reclaimed wide areas of tidal lands by damming the sea out of them and gradually building up the area thus enclosed. He increased the number of his subjects by encouraging the fishermen and craftsmen of other islands to settle in Mbau.

Chief Banuve died in one of the early epidemics that swept the islands after the arrival of the whites. At the time of his death, however, he had already raised his little island by his foresight and energy to a position of some prominence in Fiji. His traditional enemies were the people of Verata on Viti Levu and the war between the two dragged on year after year. Banuve was succeeded by a man of equal ability, Naulivou. He was the chieftain who hired Charlie Savage.

Savage had been killed in 1813. He was succeeded but not replaced by sailors from a Manila ship who mutinied, killed their captain and officers and went ashore. But there was not among them a single man of the stature of Savage and the sailors quarreled so bitterly among themselves that they killed each other off.

Mbau's war canoes, however, were very effective in their raids and the little kingdom's influence was spread by her warriors raiding distant islands.

Four years after the death of Savage a son was born to

Tanoa the younger brother of Naulivou, chief of Mbau. The boy's mother died two or three weeks after he was born and since wet nursing was abhored for it was thought that a child took with the milk the character of the donor, the baby was fed on sugarcane juice diluted with water. (The belief that a child takes with its milk the character of the donor persisted in Europe until the middle of the last century and parents looking for a wet nurse for their child were more concerned with her character than her health record. It was generally believed, for instance, that a child suckled by a woman addicted to drinking would become an alcoholic.)

The boy who was raised on sugarcane juice lived to become a cannibal, a foe of Christianity, then a Christian, and in the end established dominion over the greater part of Fiji. He was the George Washington of his country—a George Washington who strangled his wife and ate many a dinner of human flesh.

Chapter Twelve

TWENTY years after Savage's death Mbau was foremost among the petty kingdoms of Fiji. Twenty huge war canoes were moored in its harbor while others cruised on raids and collected tribute throughout the islands. A fleet of two hundred smaller canoes came and went bringing supplies to the three or four thousand inhabitants of this little Rome in Fiji. Levuka fell to Mbau and so did a whole string of islands in the middle of the Koro Sea—Ngau, Nairai, Koro, Mbatiki. The canoes of Mbau, ranging as far as the Lau Islands, fought with the Tongans for control of those islands.

When Naulivou died he was succeeded by his younger brother, Tanoa. Tanoa was short, thin and had a scowling face. He wore a bushy beard and hair and habitually smeared his cheeks and forehead with black. His brother Naulivou had once clubbed him and his head beneath the hair bore the terrible scars of the club. Perhaps for this reason Tanoa liked to dress his head in a *sala* or turban of bark cloth. The club's blow had affected his hearing and his nasal passages as well for he breathed with difficulty and was called "Old Snuff" by Europeans who met him.

His appearance did not do justice to his mentality and character. Tanoa was a man of splendid will and maintained such a household to impress his rivals that he was the envy of the other kings of Fiji. He had eight principal wives all strategically selected from his domains.

One, the mother of the boy who was to unite Fiji, was

from Mbau. The others came from Rewa, Ngau, Thakaun-drove, Lakemba, Koro, and Tailevu. He had power, through his sons, over all these places. But he was a firm and even a harsh ruler and he was not three years on the chief's stool before there were plots against him in his own kingdom.

So skillful were the plotters that Tanoa fled to Nairai and Mbau for a while was taken over by his enemies. It was his son, then called Seru, who restored his father to his kingdom. Seru pretended, in growing up, not the slightest interest in power or politics but gave the impression of caring for nothing but his self-enjoyment. Because of this he was allowed to stay on in Mbau when his father fled the tiny island.

Tanoa went into exile, first fleeing to Nairai and then to other places under his domain. However, he plotted to return to Mbau and what followed was a series of great intrigues on the scale of Lilliput for the throne of a kingdom of twenty acres.

For instance, one of the rebel chiefs on Mbau was sent to Levuka to kill Tanoa. Instead, looking to the future, he warned Tanoa of his errand and then made a great show of chasing him, leaving Tanoa to escape to Somosomo a town on the island of Taveuni northeast of Levuka. Here the chiefs of Somosomo offered him help and some of the Tongans who were present in the group, having canoes built, agreed to aid him also.

Meanwhile the French brig *L'Aimable Josephine* came to Mbau and the rebels there agreed to provide the captain with a cargo of Bêche-de-Mer if he would transport them to Somo-somo to capture Tanoa.

The French captain agreed but his expedition was a failure. The Mbau warriors fought only half-heartedly against the troops of their former king and were beaten off. The warriors enjoyed the trip, however. They had often been to sea in their huge war canoes but never on one of the great ships of the white man. They chuckled with delight at the way it heeled

88

All photographs by Rob Wright

AUTHOR AT EASE

Fijian sailing canoes constructed from hollowed logs, with sails woven from pandanus leaves, are speedy crafts that have been used by the islanders since before the coming of the white man. Modern innovations such as outboard motors and planked boats are becoming popular with the Fijians, and outrigger canoes are now found only in the outlying islands.

About 30 miles northwest of Viti
Levu, Fiji's largest island, lie
the Yasawas, a small group of beautiful islands. The village of
Matayalevu on the island of Yaqeta
is a typically picturesque spot in
this archipelago. Bligh in his
small-boat voyage after the *Bounty*
mutiny, passed through and was
chased by the hostile islanders
of the Yasawas.

A Fijian girl properly dressed for a dance has her hair combed up into a halo and her cheeks dabbed with soot.

The war-club of Thakombau, presented to Queen Victoria when Great Britain took over Fiji, now the Mace of the Legislative Council.

The bete (priest) is the most important man among the fire-walkers on the island of Mbenqa. He is in charge of everything.

The magnificent physique of the adult Fijian is shown by this warrior dressed for a "meke" or war dance. Fishing, hunting, house-building, gardening for food, and weeding with machetes are some of the many physical duties the men perform.

The famous fire-walking ceremony is performed by the people of Mbenqa, a small island about 23 miles from Suva. The Fijian name for it, Vilavilaireve, means "Jumping into the Ovens." Big stones are heated in a pit until they become white hot. Then they are levelled and the fire-walkers walk over them barefooted. No trace of burns can be found afterwards, and no satisfactory explanation of the feat has been found.

A seasea being performed by Fijian women
of Taveuni. They are clad in traditional
dress of Tapa, and are using decorated
fans in the performance of the dance, a
slow, rhythmic gesture song.

The Fijians still retain most of their traditional customs, one of the most important being the yangona ceremony. Preceding any event of importance, it is prepared with elaborate ceremonial. The drink, a mixture of the pounded root and water, is presented in coconut half-shells.

before the trade winds, climbed up and down the rigging in high glee and, nursing their bruises from the attack on Somosomo, decided that they must certainly have a ship like this.

Captain des Bureaux of *L'Aimable Josephine* was on the friendliest of terms with the two chieftains, Nanosimalua and Verani, who had led the expedition. The warriors demanded of these two chiefs that they should seize the vessel. The chiefs argued against it. They were enjoying the cheeses and wines of France in the Captain's cabin and they rather liked him. The warriors were insistent and so the chiefs gave way and the ship was taken and her captain and most of her crew massacred.

The Mbauans now possessed a real white man's ship. But they were disappointed at the other spoils that fell into their hands for there were very few muskets, and practically no trade goods aboard. Captain des Bureaux did not usually carry trade goods. He was, in fact, a rascal. He paid for pearls, tortoise shells and Bêche-de-Mer by transporting war parties about the islands, even promoting local wars for his own profit. His fellow Frenchmen described him as an outrageous villain and he had even allowed men to be cooked and eaten on his own deck. He had, then, fallen victim to his own villainy.

With a ship in their possession the warriors of Mbau decided to attack the town of Naselai on the Rewa River which had previously proved invulnerable to assault. There were enough sailors left alive to manage the vessel and these, very much hampered by the warriors who fell over each other in their efforts to assist, managed to sail the brig up the river. It was anchored off Naselai, the sailors fired the cannon and reduced the town to ruins and its defenders surrendered. The ship was heaped with spoils and headed back down the river where the Mbauans tried to navigate it themselves and ran it up on a reef. There it remained for many years though its brass cannon were taken ashore and used in tribal wars that lay ahead.

Meanwhile Tanoa remained in Somosomo (the name means "stained very black" and even among the Fijians, the people of Somosomo had a reputation for excessive cruelty and cannibalism). While there, Tanoa collected tribute from those still afraid of him and used this to buy other allies. Then, with the support of two Tongan chieftains, he moved to Rewa on Viti Levu hard by Mbau to attempt to regain his throne.

His playboy son, Seru, who had remained at Mbau was at the time hatching a plot of his own to restore his father. He got the support of the people in one quarter of the tiny island and in the middle of the night threw a war fence across the island, pinning the rebels behind it. They woke to find themselves beleaguered and under attack. Seru's warriors fired flaming arrows into the closely packed houses and the inhabitants fled in panic to the mainland. Seru then sent for his father to return to his kingdom.

From that day on Seru got a new name, Thakombau, which means "Mbau Is Destroyed." It was by that name that he rose to fame and is remembered and honored as the greatest of all the kings of Fiji.

The restoration of Tanoa to his kingdom left one unlooked-for score unsettled in the campaign that got him there. That score was the seizure of the French brig *L'Aimable Josephine*. News of the seizure of the ship and the murder of her captain had been reported in France and four years later two French corvettes, the *Astrolabe* and the *Zelee*, appeared in the Fiji Island to seek the murderers. They were under the command of Dumont d'Urville who had explored in the Fiji Islands previously. He sailed straight to Mbau, stopping only to pick up a pilot, and destroyed the town on Viti Levu from which the murderers of the captain of *L'Aimable Josephine* came.

A marked change was coming about in Fijian affairs for a new kind of white man was entering the islands. No government had cared what happened to the old beachcombers who were outlaws anyway, either escaped convicts, ship-jumpers or mutineers. But the Fijians found to their surprise that there was another kind of white man who did not fall into this class and whose life and property was protected by his government, even though that government was thousands of miles away. It was an astonishing discovery for them.

The ships that engaged in the Bêche-de-Mer trade were soon as numerous in Fiji as the sandalwood ships had been. But the waters around the islands were still uncharted. The first very incomplete chart of the whole Fiji group was published in London in 1814 and it was a hodgepodge of all the information collected by Bligh and other captains and added to this whatever could be gleaned from sandalwood traders.

This chart was perhaps more of a hazard to a captain sailing Fiji waters than no chart at all. Islands and reefs were often shown several miles out of place and any skipper who placed reliance on this chart was liable to shipwreck in the night hours.

A great number of ships were wrecked. The approach to the Fijis in those days was from Tonga in the east though the sandalwood traders had come from Australia in the southwest. The first approach took a ship through the scorpion's tail of Fiji, the Lau Group with their coral barriers and beyond them the island-studded Koro Sea with its sudden reefs rearing up from enormous depths and awash only at low tide. The list of shipwrecks was impressive.

The Nantucket trader *Oeno* was lost in 1825. The *Valedor* of Valparaiso fell to the reefs off Bura in 1828. The Salem whaler *Faun*, leaving an anchorage, missed stays while groping through a passage in the reef off Vanua Levu, drifted onto the coral and became a total wreck. A hurricane destroyed the Yankee ship *Glide* and the whaler *Shylock* also fell a victim to the Fiji reefs. So the list went on. But still the profits from Bêche-de-Mer made the hazards worthwhile.

Yankee ships from New England were the most active in the trade. These were the great days of New England sailing and captains from Salem, New London, Niantic, New Bedford and other New England ports cleared for the Fijis on a voyage around the world, often leaving their home port short of hands for the demand for seamen exceeded the supply. Farm boys from the interior were lured by adventure to the port towns and returned home to astonish their quiet neighbors with tales of cannibal feasts and cannibal battles and produced war clubs, *tapa*, carved bowls and other treasures as proof of their stories.

The ships, sailing short-handed, ran the gauntlet of Cape Hatteras and the Caribbean, picked up whatever cargo they could in Buenos Aires and then worked their way around Cape Horn through the passage that is still named after Sir Francis Drake. Some of them were driven by the current down to the Arctic ice and wrecked there. Others, unable with contrary winds and contrary currents to claw their way around the Cape, turned eastward and went around the world to Fiji by the way of the Cape of Good Hope.

The trade in Bêche-de-Mer produced profits in every stage of the voyage for the New England seamen. They took their own New England wares to South America and sold them for Spanish dollars. They traded off iron chisels and whales' teeth to the Fijians for dried sea slugs. They traded the dried sea slugs in China for silks and nankeen cloth and chinaware and the familiar blue-willow-pattern dinner sets began to make their appearance in American homes because of the daring of the Yankee seamen.

They would go anywhere, these men, carrying the flag of a new republic to the farthest ports of the world. They were largely free of the restrictions that hampered and at one time nearly killed off their British rivals who were still barred from certain portions of the world including vast areas of the South Pacific for the benefit of the East India Company. They recruited crews, when they were short, among the South Pacific Islands. A New England country boy, serving his first hitch at sea, would find as his bunkmate a dark-skinned cannibal with filed teeth and a shock of hair like a haystack.

Many Fijians, because of their love of the sea, were signed on board trading brigs and New England whalers. They made round-the-world voyages. Some of them disappeared in Australia, in China or in New England. Others came back to their home islands, decked out in uniforms fit for an admiral.

Because it was their custom to take a name that recorded any exploit they had achieved, they took English or American names on their return, so that Cokanauto, Chief of Rewa, who signed up on a whaler, returned to his homeland with the name Phillips. On his return he could speak English, was a master of American sailor talk, could also speak Tongan, Tahitian and had a smattering of Spanish and French. His voyage, however, had done nothing to improve his nature. He was as savage on his return as when he left. On one occasion he had been presented with a glass demijohn. Some of his subjects broke it. He made them eat the pieces so that they died of laceration of the intestine.

The sea slugs on which many New England shipping fortunes were built are of several varieties and quite common off the Fiji reefs. They are about ten inches long and three inches thick, are covered with little bumps like dill pickles and thickly coated with slime. They vary in color from black to dark red and the black are the most high priced in China where even today they are believed to restore sexual powers when drunk in soup.

Split open, boiled and then dried over fires of green sticks in a smokehouse or *vata*, the sea slug became a hard, leather-like object. It took several days to cure a batch in the smokehouse and the slugs had to be prevented from curling up in the process. They were measured in *piculs*—the *picul* being a Malayan word meaning the amount of weight a man could carry on his back. It was never a precise measurement but ranged between 133 and 140 pounds.

Profits were huge. One ship paid twelve hundred dollars for a cargo which was sold for twelve thousand dollars in Manila. Had she taken her cargo to China the profit would have been even greater.

The trouble, as noted, was in establishing curing stations ashore. This called for organizing divers and Fijians to work in the smokehouses. The Europeans working ashore curing Bêche-de-Mer were often murdered. Fijian chiefs were now no longer content with iron chisels, old muskets and even whales' teeth as trade items.

They reasoned that if all these things were on the ships there was nothing to stop them taking ship and cargo themselves. The Yankee brig *Charles Doggett* anchored off Ono Island in September of 1834 was the victim of such a plot. The local chief planned to seize the ship. The mate and several of the crew were busy in the *vata* house when it was suddenly surrounded by warriors who set the building on fire. As the men rushed out to escape the flames, they were clubbed. Ten were killed in this manner, eight of them Americans. The mate and a boy were clubbed and speared when they were within a few feet of the ship's boat on the beach.

The beachcomber, Paddy Connell, who survived in the Fijis under some special Irish charm, was an eye witness to these murders. Seeing the slaughter on the beach, the *Charles Doggett* opened fire with her cannon and was able to get away.

There was another attack on the English brig *Sir David Ogilvie*, commanded by a Captain Hutchins. Hutchins was an old hand in the Fiji trade but he was suddenly clubbed on his own quarterdeck by a Fiji chief standing beside him. Immediately he fell, Fijians in canoes around the ship swarmed aboard and seized her. But Hutchins had taken the precaution of putting some muskets in the foretop. The man on duty there grabbed a musket and started firing down on the decks. The Fijians, taken by surprise by this fire from above, left the ship in panic and the vessel was saved. The chieftain who had murdered the captain was shot sitting in the captain's cabin.

With the Bêche-de-Mer ships came the whalers. Again they were for the most part from New England though some came from Port Jackson in Australia. Sperm whale abounded off the Fijis, being most plentiful during the winter months of August and September. They followed a migration pattern which the New Englanders soon discovered. They came to the warm tropical waters to breed and then migrated south in the Antarctic spring of January and February to feed on the plankton which abounded at that season off the ice shelf.

The whalers followed the sperm and in the 1830's as many as one a week were calling on the Fiji Islands. The whalermen had fine goods for trading in the teeth of the sperm which they caught. With these they obtained ship's stores or Bêche-de-Mer for their captains did not limit the profits of their voyage to the taking of whales. Because of the whales' teeth on board, whalers were especially liable to attack in the Fijis and the mate and a boat's crew of the Port Jackson ship *Nimrod* were kidnapped and held to ransom for fifty whale's teeth by the Fijians. The chief who arranged this kidnapping was the same who had killed ten men from the *Charles Doggett*.

These attacks on shipping could not be allowed to go unpunished and it was not long before the Fijians were facing the warships of the white men's governments. Prominent among these were the warships of the United States of America.

But before this kind of action was taken Christian missionaries arrived in the Fiji Islands. They were earnest and devout men prepared to sacrifice their lives to convert the most fearsome cannibals of the South Seas. They came in fear and trembling. But they came anyway. They were in many ways splendid men.

Chapter Thirteen

THE first Christian missionaries to arrive in the Fijis were not European but Tahitian. Their names were Hanea and Atai and they had been sent to Tonga on their way to Fiji by the London Missionary Society under John Williams. When they arrived in Tonga they found no ship to take them to Fiji for four years. They did not bother to learn the Tongan language finding that the Tongans could understand Tahitian. In 1830 they went to Fiji making their headquarters on the tiny island of Oneata in the Lau or eastern group. They lived there under the protection of a chieftain who came from Tonga with them and had also been to both Tahiti and Sydney. His name was Takai.

Tonga had been quite largely Christianized by this time and the islands of the group united under King George who was himself a Christian. He was a remarkable administrator and his Tongan name was Tabou. The Tongans were at this time regularly visiting the eastern Fijis and formed a big part of the population of some of those islands. They held the Fijians in great respect for their prowess in building canoes, in weaving matting and making pottery and in war. They even admired them, though they did not admit this openly, for their cannibalism, and some of the Tongans took to cannibalism themselves to prove they were as tough as the Fijians.

The eastern islands of Fiji were then, to some degree, an extension of Tonga and when the first European missionaries came to the Fijis they settled also in the Tongan area at Tabou, a town on the island of Lakemba named after the Tongan king. The chieftain there, Tui Nayau, welcomed them, provided them with houses but said he wasn't interested in becoming a Christian though he would not stop them preaching.

Without their knowledge the missionaries, William Cross and David Kargill, were lucky in their choice of Lakemba as a place to start their work. To the east of the island lies the reef on which the *Argo* was wrecked. Its crew and passengers were the first Europeans known to have landed in the Fiji Islands. Most of them were killed and eaten and among the victims were two passengers who wore dark clothing. After these two had been eaten a terrible sickness broke out among the islanders. The islanders suspected that the gods of the dark-clothed strangers were angry with them. When, therefore, the missionaries arrived, dressed in dark clothing, they were, though they did not know it, protected against being eaten.

This did not, however, make their task any easier. They were not long on the island before the native priests were promising that the island would be flooded and the missionaries and their new religion swept into the sea. Then they prophesied that the island would be turned inside out and everybody killed. A new temple was to be built. It was the custom to bury a man alive at the foot of the posts supporting the temple roof and the priests said that the man chosen for this would be a Christian while others would be killed and eaten. But the missionaries and their converts were unafraid and when none of these things happened they gained stature among the Fijians.

The chief at Lakemba was in a difficult position. He dared not expel the missionaries who were making converts among his people because they came to him under the protection of King George of Tonga. He dared not become a Christian himself, thus joining them, because this might bring down on him the wrath of the terrible king of Mbau to whom he was subject. He therefore pleaded with the missionaries to settle in the land of some greater chief, and assured them that if some really big chieftain were converted they would gain, at one stroke, thousands of converts.

There was some sense to these arguments and the two missionaries decided that one of them must go to Mbau. The Reverend Cross was the man chosen. But he arrived when Mbau was celebrating the restoration of Tanoa as king. A big feast was being prepared and to his horror the missionary discovered that two bodies were already cooking in the oven. The Reverend Cross saw Tanoa's son, Seru, now called Thakombau, who received him with civility and even gave him a place on the tiny island on which to build a house.

But the missionary did not feel under the circumstances that his work would be successful and being invited by the king of Rewa to come to his territory accepted this offer. Here he nearly died of typhoid and it was David Whippy of New Hampshire who saved him. After that the mission prospered though Mr. Cross was often stoned and on one occasion had his house burned down.

It was not long before some of the chieftains began to want missionaries among them. To have a white man in his town was, of course, a matter of prestige for a chief or a king. In the case of the missionaries there were further gains. They had a few trade goods such as knives, iron pots and hatchets which they gave to the islanders and the chiefs coveted these things. Again the white men's ships rarely failed to call at a town where a missionary was stationed, bringing increasing trade. And so the powerful King Tui Thakau of Somosomo on the island of Taveuni, lying off the southeast of Vanua Levu came to Lakemba to ask for a missionary. He brought his two sons with him and argued potently.

"The chief here," he said, "is not very powerful. He has only a few people and they are poor and he cannot practice what you teach without the consent of his overlords. If you will come to us, we will allow you to teach our children. We will ourselves listen to your doctrine to find out whether it is true or false. It is a disgrace that you sit here with these small chiefs and ignore us who are so much greater."

The king's eldest son, Tui Kilakila, talked to the missionary who at that time was the Reverend David Cargill, for some hours about Christianity. At the end of that time the Reverend Cargill asked Tui Kilakila, whose name might be translated as "The Chief Who Guesses," whether he believed the teachings of Christianity to be true.

"True!" cried Tui Kilakila. "Everything that comes from the white man's country is true. His muskets are true, and his gunpowder is true, and therefore his religion must be true!"

Still the missionaries were doubtful about going to Somosomo. The place was one of terror. Cannibalism was more widely practiced in Somosomo than anywhere else in Fiji. Death lay in the king's look and feasts of human flesh in which a score of men might be eaten were not uncommon. On the other hand, there was no doubt that the king of Somosomo held enormous influence over other chiefs and his sons were *vasus* over all the dominions of powerful Mbau. These arguments prevailed and two missionaries, the Reverend Hunt and the Reverend Lyth, were sent to Somosomo with their wives and children.

They arrived in the midst of horror. The king's youngest son, Ra Biti, had gone with a fleet of canoes to some other islands and the missionaries had hardly landed before news reached Somosomo that he was dead. He had, in fact, been killed and eaten. The son of so powerful a king could not be allowed to go unaccompanied into the other world. Several women were immediately set apart to be strangled so they could accompany him.

99

The missionaries pleaded for their lives. The most they could achieve was to delay the strangling until news of the young prince's death was confirmed. When confirmation was obtained, the protests of the missionaries were in vain. Sixteen women were immediately strangled and the bodies buried within a few yards of the missionaries' house.

This was the beginning of the ordeal of the missionaries in Somosomo. Not long after the Reverend Hunt, looking through the open window of his little schoolhouse, saw eleven dead men dragged by their necks into the town. They were cut up there and then, and cooked. The smell of the flesh from the ovens filled the mission house and afterwards the people of Somosomo became increasingly hostile to the Christians and refused to sell them food.

They boasted that they would kill and eat them, too, and there were many nights when a big feast was going on in the town that the missionaries and their families expected at any moment to be dragged out and clubbed. They spent such nights in prayer, their children kneeling with them.

These men were all from England and were Wesleyans. But their first governmental help came from Commodore Charles Wilkes of the United States. Because of the growing American trade in Fiji waters, he was sent with a squadron of ships to survey the Fijis. He called at Somosomo and after talking with the missionaries told Tui Kilakila to allow no harm to come to the missionaries or he would be very severely punished. He also made the Tui agree to a treaty whereby vessels visiting his dominions would not be molested.

Wilkes, seeing the plight of the missionaries at Somosomo, offered to transport them and their families to any other part of the islands they wished to go. But they would not leave, feeling, though they lived in fear of their lives, that they might yet be able to do some good work.

The first missionaries had brought to Fiji a little printed book in the Fiji language, the book being printed in Tonga.

It was only four pages. Later the missionaries got a printing press and were able to print the gospels in the Fiji language.

To do this they had first to provide an alphabet, for Fijian had never before been written down. The immediate problem was that in the Fiji tongue vowels always follow consonants and there is no such thing as two consonants coming together as in English. Letter combinations such as "th" and "ng" were likely to be pronounced by Fijians, if the English alphabet were used, as "teh" and "neg." The missionaries, therefore, used the English alphabet but assigned to some letters the sound of two letters. Thus the letter "c" stood for "th" and the letter "d" for "nd" and "b" for "mb." As an illustration Bau is so spelled in Fijian but is pronounced Mbau and Cakobau is properly pronounced "thakombau." It will be seen that phonetic spelling has been used in this book.

At the mission schools the Fijians, young and old, loved to study reading and writing. For all their savagery and dark ways they were among the most intelligent people of the South Seas and indeed one of the few people with whom a European could hold a conversation of some length that did not consist of childish trivialities.

Eventually the missionaries had to withdraw from Somosomo. They left not from fear, though surrounded by horrors, but because the people resisted conversion and they felt they should go to others who were more disposed to accept Christianity.

They dared not, however, tell Tui Kilakila that they were leaving. Secretly they got their pitiful valuables together, even removing the screws from the door hinges by night to take away with them. They were miserably poor and a screw had value. They were expecting the ship *Triton* to call and had everything prepared for her arrival, including the complete dismantling of the house.

All their possessions were smuggled on board the *Triton* by night. When most of the valuables were on board the missionaries went to the king and told him that they were leaving since he had closed his mind so hard against their preaching. The king made no reply. They went away unsure whether they had done any good at all in Somosomo.

Later they learned some good had been achieved for other Fijians reported that Somosomo had changed. The people were less cruel and bloody. It was a small gain but a significant one.

Unfortunately the patience and charity which the missionaries showed toward the cannibals did not extend to other missionaries of differing faiths. Protestant and Catholic were embittered one against the other and the Protestant missionaries took comfort when Catholic priests were discountenanced in their teachings and the same went for the Catholic priests. The separated brethren were separated indeed, and the savages of Fiji were puzzled to discover that there was not one true religion among the white men but several, bitterly antagonistic toward each other.

A more generous spirit in religious matters was indeed shown by a pagan Fiji priest. The island of Ono had been subjected to an epidemic that decimated the population. Food was short and the people, after making sacrifices to their gods, got no relief.

A canoe was sent to Lakemba, a hundred and fifty miles away, carrying tribute to that island to which Ono was subject. The chief from Ono, while at Lakemba, heard of Christianity and the worship of a true god whose name was Jehovah. He went back to Ono with only that information about Christianity, plus the fact that Jehovah had to be worshipped every seventh day. He spread the news and the islanders decided to turn in their distress to Jehovah for help.

They set aside one day for his worship, washed themselves, put on their best clothes and assembled in a spirit house, or temple, but they did not know how to conduct a service or even how to pray. In their own religion there were no serv-

ices and only the priests spoke to the gods. They went, therefore, to one of their pagan priests and explained the problem
to him. He agreed to try to help them and came to the house
where they were gathered and prayed somewhat as follows:

"Lord Jehovah, here are your people. They worship you.
I do not worship you but another god. But since these people
trust in you, bless them, keep them from harm and do them
good."

The old priest then went back to his own temple having
conducted in a spirit of charity the first Christian service in
Ono. He continued to oblige these people by holding services for them until a missionary arrived to take over. He
himself remained a pagan.

Chapter Fourteen

THE island of Mbengga is the Holy Land of old Fiji. It lies south of Viti Levu, a beautiful mountainous island with fertile valleys in the deep ridges between the mountains. It is encircled on the south and east by a massive reef and there are coral heads and rocks to the north and west but a deep passage between these and Viti Levu.

Mbengga is the Holy Land of Fiji because during the Flood it was on the mountains of this island that the Fijian Noah and his people were saved.

In the folklore of Fiji there is a detailed story of the great flood which inundated the whole world. The Fiji story closely parallels that of the Bible, the flood resulting from a deluge brought about by the anger of their supreme god. According to the story two boys spitefully killed Turukawa a favorite bird belonging to the supreme serpent god, Ndengei. The boys were the grandsons of Ndengei but instead of apologizing for killing the bird, mocked him and defied him to punish them.

His revenge was to cause thick masses of clouds to appear over the earth so that they blotted out the sun and when there was no light left on earth, because of the thickness of the clouds, the clouds burst, pouring their contents in a deluge upon the earth. All was submerged under the water. The two offenders had built themselves a high tower which seems to correspond to the Tower of Babel but the waters rose higher and higher and they were in danger of being drowned. At last they cried out to another god, who pitying them, told them to make a raft and float it on the water where, he promised, they would be saved. They did this and embarked on the raft with six friends.

After many days floating on the dark water the raft touched the peak of one mountain that had not been submerged—the Ararat of Fiji. The mountain was the highest on the island of Mbengga and here the survivors stayed until the floodwaters subsided, and from Mbengga, repopulated the whole of Fiji. For this reason the people of Mbengga stand first in Fijian rank and are called "the people who are subject only to god."

The islanders are reverenced even to this day, partially because of the story of the flood but also because the people of one village on the island have the ability to walk on fire. They received this gift also from a god and in the following manner.

Many centuries ago there lived in the mountain village of Na Vakeisese a famous storyteller who was called Dredre. He used to entertain the villages every night with his tales and they brought him gifts of food in payment for his entertainment. One night, after he had told them a particularly splendid story, they asked him what gift he would like in payment.

"When your warriors go out in the morning to hunt, let them bring me the first quarry they catch," said Dredre.

One of the warriors, a chieftain named Tui-Na-Iviqalita, went fishing in a mountain stream and caught a snakefish or eel. When he pulled it out of the mud at the bottom of the river, however, the eel turned into a tiny man and Tui knew that he had captured a god.

"I am pleased to have captured you," he said, "for now I will take you to Dredre the storyteller and he will be well rewarded for his excellent tale."

"What will he do with me?" asked the god.

"He will kill you and eat you," replied Tui.

"Let me go," cried the little man, "and I will make you the greatest warrior of your tribe."

"That is a very foolish thing to say," replied Tui. "You offer me something I already possess. Of all the people of the Sawau tribe to which I belong I am the greatest warrior."

"Let me go," said the little man, "and I will make you the greatest hunter in your tribe."

"I begin to doubt the intelligence of gods," said Tui, "Have I not captured you, who are a god, and does this not make me the greatest hunter of my tribe?"

"Let me go," said the little man, "and I will make you the greatest lover among your people."

"Just before I give you to Dredre, the storyteller, to be cooked and eaten, I will take you around my village and you will see all the young girls smiling at me and I will show you some twenty or thirty of my wives," said Tui. "It seems to me that the gods, if they are all like you, only promise a man what he already possesses." The little man was by now desperate. Tui was about to fling him in his basket and carry him down to the village when he made one more attempt at saving his life.

"There is one thing you do not possess that I can give to you," the god said. "You think that you can cook me. But that is not so, for I am impervious to fire. No oven can destroy me and if you will let me go back into the lovely soft mud of the river where I can become a snakefish again, I will give you also the gift of being invulnerable to flames."

At this Tui was interested but did not believe the god and said so.

"To prove what I have to say," said the god, "why don't you build a big oven here and heat it as hot as you can and I will jump into it and it will not hurt me. Then I will call you to jump in, too, and if you have the courage to do so, you will find that the fire will not hurt you."

A Fiji oven of the kind in which feasts are cooked to this day consists of a pit four feet deep and as many as twenty feet across. It is usually dug in a circular shape, the earth from

106

the pit being thrown around the lip to form a bank. Into this are put logs to a height of two or three feet. These are fired and the logs are covered with round boulders such as may be obtained from the bed of a river. This oven, which is more of a furnace, burns for several hours until the stones are white hot. The food, wrapped in leaves, is then put on top of the stones and covered with earth and is thus cooked.

This was the oven that Tui prepared for the little god and when the stones were white hot the little fellow walked onto them and stood in the middle of the oven and called to Tui to come and join him. Tui was indeed the bravest warrior of his tribe for after only a moment's hesitation, he stepped onto the stones and found to his astonishment that his feet were not burned and did not even feel the heat of the white hot rocks.

"This is a gradual process," said the god. "Your feet are now impervious to fire. Now let us dig a hole in these hot stones down to the blazing logs below and we will both crawl into it when your whole body will be proof against the flames. Look. I will show you."

The god wriggled between two seething boulders and Tui could see him sitting quite comfortably on a burning log at the base of the oven.

"Come out of there," he cried. "This is enough for me. I can see no occasion when I will want to bury myself in an oven and I am quite happy to be able to just walk over the top."

"The day might come when someone would want to cook you, as you say the storyteller will cook me," cautioned the god.

"When the day comes that I am to be cooked," said Tui, "I will have been clubbed first and dead and it would not be fair to deprive my killer of my meat. So come on out and I will set you free. But first of all I would like to be able to teach the people of my tribe to walk on fire."

"That is a little beyond our bargain," said the god. "But

since I have taken a liking to you I will tell you the secret. However, you must not make it generally known but convey it only to a selected band of men whom you can trust and who will in turn tell it to others."

He then told Tui how to teach others to walk on fire, and so the people of Tui's village learned the secret, the god was set free, and the storyteller, Dredre, was cheated of his proper reward for his story. This, however, is not infrequently the case in the literary profession.

I determined to visit Mbengga and, although I did not see the women of Kandavu call the turtles out of the sea, at least witness the fire walking of the islanders. This time I was fortunate, saw a performance, and took motion pictures of it.

The circumstances were as follows. On my second visit to the Fiji Islands I called on Rob who immediately called Captain Stan Brown of the one hundred-ton diesel motor-sailor *Maroro*. I knew Stan well. He is one of the finest sailors in the South Seas. He has followed the sea since boyhood and the *Maroro*, in which he now trades between the islands and takes charter parties to distant places, was at one time the royal yacht of Queen Salote of Tonga. Stan had taken me to the eastern Fijis on my previous trip of which I will tell later, and had hardly sat down before he mentioned that he was due to sail that night in the *Maroro* to Mbengga.

"What for?" I asked.

"There is to be a fire walking ceremony in honor of an official at Lautoka on the eastern side of Viti Levu," he said. "The fire walkers have asked me whether I will take them there by sea. They have to take all their equipment with them."

"Can I come?" I asked.

"If you can be aboard by midnight," said Stan.

I checked out of my hotel without ever having slept in the bed and put my bags on board the *Maroro*. We sailed in the early hours for Mbengga to pick up the firewalkers.

108

Mbengga is one of the most beautiful islands of the Fijis. Its mountains, which are volcanic, form grotesque shapes against the tropical sky. At times, peaks like giant's heads show clearly and then dissolve in white mists that sift gently over them.

The reef around the island is formidable, with but a single passage through it. Once inside, however, the lagoon is quiet and the anchorage good and the water was of that incredible blue to which I will never become accustomed. We anchored off Mbengga in the morning and I went ashore to the village of the fire walkers.

One of the headmen of the village met me and showed me around. The people lived in the pandanus-thatched huts of Fiji, scattered under the graceful coconut palms and with a stupendous mountain rushing up behind their village. On the lower flank of the mountain is a school and the approach is so steep that the path to it goes upward in a zigzag. The women were dressed in the long petticoat and knee-length outer frock which is the costume of Fiji. The men, alas, wore khaki shorts and the kind of flowered shirts sold to tourists in Hawaii. Nobody seemed able to speak English except the *Buli*, Timothy, whose name in Fijian would be spelled Timoci. I am sure the children could speak English for they went to school where they learn both English and Fijian. Whenever I tried to talk to them they just stared at me and then giggled. The women giggled, too. They were dark and plump and comely—a happy people who seem to have no anxieties. At each hut I passed they peeped out at me so that a window would be filled with five or six smiling and wholesome faces.

There was not a great deal to see in the village that I had not seen before. It began to rain so I went back on board the *Maroro*. I was hardly back before the fire walkers started to bring the materials for their ceremony out to the ship.

First they swam huge rafts of logs from the beach out to the boat. They bring their own wood for the fire and their own boulders. This is not because the wood burns at a lower temperature or the boulders have some special quality which prevents them getting really hot. It is because Mbengga is sacred and so to some degree is the wood and the stones that are used in the ceremony. The islanders are tremendous swimmers. One man could swim a raft of logs weighing a quarter of a ton out to the *Maroro* against wind and tide and push it along at a good speed. The logs brought alongside were hoisted in the *Maroro*'s tackle onto the decks and stowed there. They were five or six feet long and with a diameter of up to six inches.

The wood was green and water soaked and I doubted that it could be set on fire. After the logs came the boulders, round river boulders, brownish in color, extremely heavy and of about the size of cannon shot. These were also hoisted on board and stored on the decks.

A stocky, elderly Fijian with gray hair and formidable features attended to the stowing. He was the witch doctor or *bete*. It was he who would lead the men of the village over the seething stones in their ceremony. After the boulders, outriggers came out with large quantities of green stuff aboard. Some of it was swamp grass, but Timothy pointed to some fernlike vines and said, "*Drau-ni-balabala*. The sacred vines."

Drau-ni-balabala means the leaf of a species of tree fern, Cyathea lunulata. The juice of the stem is used by the Fijians to cure headache. The scales from the outer bark are used for stuffing pillows, and the heart of the plant is eaten in times of food shortage.

But *drau-ni-balabala* has a special use in connection with the fire walking. Circlets of the plant are tied around the ankles of the fire walkers and according to the promise of the god to Tui will prevent the legs of the performers being burned above the anklets of vines. Their feet are, of course, proof against the heat.

A purification rite must be performed by the fire walkers

before the ceremony. Two weeks ahead of the fire walking the men who are to take part in it move into a special house where they live together. They are forbidden, under a tabu, to have any intercourse with women and they eat special foods, recite, I believe, certain invocations and are forbidden to eat coconut or any food derived from coconut. Timothy told me all these details of fire walking.

"If you would undergo our purification ceremony and do all the things that the fire walkers must do to prepare themselves, I would lead you out onto the stones myself and you would not be hurt," he said with great sincerity. The proposition was attractive, for no European, and indeed nobody who is not from Mbengga, can walk on the stones.

"Timothy," I replied, "my feet are so tender that I cannot even walk along a cold-pebbled beach without my shoes on."

"If you believed and did what is necessary, you could walk over the stones," said Timothy. But I had not that amount of faith.

When all were aboard, the *Maroro* sailed and as she headed for the passage through the reef, the fire walkers of Mbengga and those who accompanied them, lined the ship's rail and sang "Isa Lei," the haunting Fijian song of farewell. There was a great nostalgia and melancholy in the scene. The deep voices of the men echoed back to them softly across the lagoon from the mountains of their island. "Isa Lei" is one of the most beautiful songs of farewell I have ever heard and the Fijians have magnificent voices, especially in choral singing. Indeed, I believe they are the equivalent of the Welsh, who are even greater singers than the Irish though that seems impossible.

We were twenty hours fetching Lautoka on western Viti Levu. This part of the island is to leeward and markedly different from the windward coast. The moisture-sodden winds from the east are leached of their rain by the mountains before they reach the west coast which is much drier. Its mountains, then, are not covered with jungle growth but are bare like the mountains of California. There is a dry desert tang in the air, though, during the rainy season, there is sufficient rainfall to raise sugarcane which is grown in large quantities in western Viti Levu.

The occasion of the fire walking was to honor a British official who had done a great deal for the welfare of the Fijians in the Lautoka area. They, in return, had determined to present him with their highest honor—a whale's tooth. No expenditure of money or adroit politiking can obtain this honor from the Fijians. They give it only to those whose work attests to real public service and nobility of character and so the presentation is always formal and attended by the ancient ceremonies of the people.

Prime among these ceremonies is the preparation of *yangona* which is so sacred a rite in Fiji that the formal serving of the drink is never done for mere display. Indeed, it partakes of the nature of a sacrament.

Yangona is the Fiji word for what is elsewhere in the South Seas called *kava* or *ava*. The drink is prepared from the root of the pepper plant, Piper latiforlum or Piper methysticum. Taken in large quantities it is intoxicating but it is a narcotic and not an alcohol. Those intoxicated by it become drowsy and melancholy but in reasonable doses *yangona* is said to be an excellent tonic for the kidneys.

Old hands in the South Seas drink a bowl or two of *yangona* if they have had a heavy evening of alcohol drinking and claim that this offsets the ill effect of the alcohol.

At the Lautoka ceremony there was first of all a club dance by the Fijians such as they used to stage before battle to mock their enemies. The dancers dressed in skirts of pandanus leaves and glistening with coconut oil, went through all the mimicry of a battle with war clubs and when at the finale they brought their clubs down on the ground, the earth shook a little.

The *yangona* was mixed in a huge wooden bowl which

has a plaited cord of sinnet or coconut fiber attached to it on one side. At the other end of this cord was a large white cowrie shell. The huge bowl was placed before the guest of honor, but about a hundred feet away, and the cord with cowrie shell stretched toward him. In the old days it was instant death to pass between this shell and the person being honored and even today no one would commit such a breach of courtesy.

The *yangona* was mixed in the bowl with water, the lees being strained by fibers of hibiscus which were scooped through the mixture to capture them. Each movement of this scooping is performed in a special manner and men are trained from boyhood to strain the *yangona*. When it was ready for serving a huge Fijian, who held the office of cupbearer and was dressed in a skirt of cloth made of paper (which is called *masi* in Fiji and *tapa* elsewhere) received a half coconut shell of the *yangona* which he held with great reverence in both hands.

He was a magnificent man, weighing perhaps two hundred twenty pounds and about six feet two in height. He knelt, facing the guest of honor, with the coconut shell of *yangona* held before him in outstretched arms. Very slowly, and in a complete silence, he rose to his full height and advanced to the guest of honor and presented him with the *yangona* which had to be drunk in one draft.

I have never seen any ceremony more dignified and reverent. As soon as the bowl was drained the rest clapped their hands and shouted some ritual words, then the other guests were served according to their degree.

Next the chieftan presented the whale's tooth. It was about five inches long, an inch and a half in diameter at its large end, and yellow with age. The chieftain held it in his hands and made an address in Fijian which was punctuated by a chanting shout from the others around. He then presented it to the official. But it was returned to the chieftain for the

113

presentation is spiritual and the tooth itself remains in the hands of the Fijians. Too many, alas, of these *quasi*—sacred whales' teeth—were taken from the Fijis during World War II as war souvenirs.

Meanwhile for eighteen hours the oven or fire pit over which the fire walkers would walk had been burning away. I inspected it several times and took some eight-mm movie footage of it. To do this I had to use a telephoto lens. The stones on top of the blazing logs were so hot that it was impossible to get within fifteen feet of the pit. The stones were indeed exploding from the heat. While I took my film, fragments whizzed past me like machine-gun bullets. There was no doubt, then, of the intense heat of the boulders.

I was amused to find a St. John's ambulance unit standing by and so were the fire walkers. Timothy, their chief, said that the ambulance was there, not for the fire walkers, but in case any of the spectators fainted during the ceremony. I asked him whether he had ever done the fire walking himself. He said he had and unwillingly.

The islanders had been invited to New Zealand to put on a performance. When they arrived the *bete* or witch doctor announced that there were not enough men to give an impressive show and so Timothy, who went along as a sort of manager, must walk over the stones. He had never done this before and pleaded that he was not worthy of the honor. The *bete* replied grimly that while he might not be worthy, he would make him so. Timothy, then, had to walk.

"When I approached the pit," he said, "the hot, dry air seared my lungs so it was difficult to breathe. I was sure I was going to be horribly mutilated. I watched the *bete* step onto the stones, which were exploding with heat, and walk around the pit, and I watched the others step behind him. I stepped onto the boulders myself, half in a daze, and expected to be terribly burned. But to my astonishment I did not feel even the slightest heat on the soles of my feet. I assure you again that if you would submit to the purification ceremony you could do it yourself."

"Timothy," I replied, "I thank God at this moment that I am not subject to the orders of the *bete*."

At noon I made another inspection of the pit. The stones which had been a brownish color were now blackened on the bottom and white on top. They were still exploding and I picked up a fragment (when it had cooled off) as a souvenir. The white-haired, grim-visaged *bete* took a look at the flaming pit, grunted, and moved off.

"It isn't hot enough yet," said Timothy.

Chapter Fifteen

THE oven had been burning twenty hours or more before the *bete* decided that it was hot enough for the men to walk over it. A huge crowd had by now gathered around in specially constructed stands to watch the fire walking. The fire walkers had tied the circlet of vines around their ankles and were dressed in the costume the ceremony demanded. They wore skirts of pandanus leaf or some other long leaf, but these were stained in yellow and black, a coloring not used by other Fijians. They had leis of flowers around their necks, strung on pandanus fiber dyed purple, and their hair was dressed in Fijian style, brushed upwards and made to stand in this position by some special preparation.

First of all, however, the still blazing logs had to be pulled out of the pit. This was done by the fire walkers' using long green poles with lassos of vines called *walai* on the end.

They seemed to enjoy this work immensely. Four or five men would get hold of a pole, snare a log in the lasso, go through a pantomime of vigorous tugging and then dash away from the pit with a mere chip of smouldering wood caught in the lasso.

They laughed and everybody laughed. I think this was part of their mockery of fire over which they had achieved supremacy. But they also pulled out burning brands three and four feet in length and dashed off with them at the end of their poles, laughing and shouting with excitement. When a piece of one of these logs fell off, a man would kick it ahead of him contemptuously as if it were a football. If it were too big to be treated in this manner, he would pick it up, unhurriedly, in his hands and carry it out of the arena. There were no fear or nervousness among the men; no sign of anxiety over the ordeal they were to undergo.

When all the burning logs had been extracted, leaving only the white-hot stones that were still exploding, the *bete* called for the *waqa-bala-bala*. This is the trunk of a tree fern and it is said to contain the spirit of the god who protects the men from the fire. It was laid with some reverence by the side of the pit. With the removal of the burning logs the seething boulders had settled into a cone which it was necessary to level. The *waqa-bala-bala* was then placed over the stones with two large vines attached to each end, and, using the "spirit of the god," the stones were leveled in the pit by dragging the tree trunk over them.

This leveling was done to a great deal of joyous shouting rather reminiscent of the American tribal practice of shouting "go, go, go" at football games. When the stones were leveled the *bete* went to the edge of the pit in a profound silence that settled over the audience, stepped deliberately onto them with his bare feet to see that they were firm and none of his men would stumble as a result of one slipping.

Despite the demonstration they had already given of being able to pick up burning logs in their hands, the god had promised protection from burning only for their feet, and if one of them fell as a result of a boulder slipping, he would be horribly burned all over his body. When the *bete* was satisfied that the stones were firmly placed, he went away to an area at the side of the arena where the fire walkers were gathered.

Through the courtesy of the high chief in charge of the whole ceremony, Roko Tui Ba, to whom I was introduced by Stan, I was given a privileged position at the fire walking ceremony to photograph it. I was not held back to the spectator area but allowed to approach the pit as close as the heat and consideration for the other spectators would decently permit.

I got my camera ready and waited. A silence hard as steel settled over the whole area. Then, without a sound and in a reverent procession, the fire walkers led by the *bete* approached the pit. There was a slight wind blowing and just before they reached the edge, a tuft of dried grass was blown over the pit. It struck the edge, was lifted up by the wind, fell in the center and immediately burst into flames and was consumed in a moment. That was the heat of the boulders on which these men were to walk.

There was no hesitation among them and no sign on their faces of being in a state of hypnotism. They appeared grave and reverent and when the *bete* reached the lip of the pit which was too hot for me to have approached, he shouted, "*Vutu-o*," and stepped, without hesitation, onto the boulders.

The shout of *vutu-o* means, "let us cross." He made a complete circle of the furnace followed by his men who were not bunched up for comfort but walked a couple of feet behind each other. There was no hurry, no wincing, no anxiety except among the spectators. They completed their circle over the white-hot boulders which seared the grass of their skirts and stepped out again. And then there was a thunderous applause from the several hundred spectators who had watched the feat.

The ceremony, however, was not yet over. As soon as the circle of the pit had been made a great shout was raised and bundles of grass and leaves were tossed onto the stones causing an immense cloud of smoke to rise, in itself testimony to the heat of the boulders. These, I understand, were offerings to the fire god who, deprived of his right to burn the fire walkers, still demanded a sacrifice to appease his hunger.

Then, everybody, fire walkers and those who had accompanied them as helpers, jumped into the pit and began stamp-

118

ing the green stuff around while others shoveled earth on top. Some of this greenery caught fire and as impressive as the fire walking itself was the impunity with which the Fijians stamped around on the burning, smouldering earth and bundles of leaves. They were enveloped in smoke so that only their heads and torsos were visible and they looked like so many demons exulting in a furnace.

When this cover had been put down to their satisfaction, four baskets of roots called *vasili* were put into the oven to be cooked. These also are a kind of offering to the fire god taking the place of the fire walkers. The pit was then covered over with earth until the roots were cooked and they were later eaten by the fire walkers.

I wanted to look at the feet of one of the men who had gone over the hot stones and did so. There was not the slightest sign of burning on the soles which were thickly skinned as are the feet of all people accustomed to walking about without shoes. I have to admit that the feet of most Fijians are so tough that they can walk on sharp coral with impunity. But even assuming that there was such a thickness of skin on the soles of the fire walker's feet, that they could not feel the heat of the boulders, one could expect to see burn marks on the skin. There were none. Many medical men who have witnessed the fire walking ceremony have examined the feet of the fire walkers and concluded that however thick the skin, such heat would penetrate to the nerves causing intense pain. In any case the calloused soles would show marks of burning. But none have ever found such marks and there is no scientific explanation of the ability of the men of Mbengga to walk on fire.

The gift, alas, is likely to be lost. I was told that since it contains at least a smattering of heathenism, it is frowned upon by the Christian church. Timothy told me that few of the younger people are prepared to walk on the boulders and he believed that in a generation or so there would be no more fire walking by the people of the sacred island of Mbengga.

Perhaps also the women of Kandavu will forget the princess and her daughter who were turned into turtles and summon them no more from the sea; and perhaps the people of Kambara will forget how to build their great war canoes with a ceremony for every piece of rope used to lash them together—a ceremony for the cutting of the hull, for the installation of the weather boards, for the stepping of the mast and the raising of the sails.

This may be progress but it is also sadness. There is an increase of this sadness in the world as we are cut off from the tradition and beliefs of our ancestors. We grow increasingly efficient and increasingly lost and lonely. The people of Mbengga are able to walk on fire, but I know of no Christians who are capable of walking on water. There is food for thought in this.

Chapter Sixteen

THE island of Malolo lies to the west of Viti Levu off the Nandi River. It is really two islands, Malolo itself, and Malololeilei, meaning "Little Malolo." But they are joined, with any fall of the tide, by a sandy peninsula.

Two generous bays sweep into the sand at this point, the one on the western side being one of the most beautiful bays I have ever seen. It is a tremendous half circle of sand which gleams in the sunlight and slopes gently into the limpid water, so clear that in ten or fifteen feet you can see not only pebbles but the shadows they cast on the bottom.

I visited Malolo with Stan on the *Maroro*. During the last war troops were stationed on the island. It is, though not necessarily because of this, one of the most miserable of the Fiji islands, despite its natural beauties. The *Maroro* could not come in close because of the inevitable coral shelf so we took the dinghy as far as we might and then waded over the coral to go ashore.

Where the edge of the shelf met the sea a villager was diving for fish. He was huge and dark and wore little plastic goggles. He was the only man in the village I saw working. When we arrived ashore it was to find a village not of pandanus thatch but of squalid clapboards and corrugated iron roofs. We went, as is the custom in the Fijis, to the house of the chief to ask his permission to visit his island. He invited us into his clapboard hut and we squatted on the floor and made a gift of *yangona* roots.

The gift is always made with a little speech in Fijian which goes something like this: "I have come to your island in the hope that you will allow me, out of your generosity, to visit among your people and you will extend to me your protection while I am with you. I do not claim to be worthy of this honor but hope in the bigness of your heart that you will grant it to me. I have brought with me a gift of no significance and certainly I do not pretend that it is something worthy of your acceptance. Yet I hope you will ignore the poorness of my gift and accept it from me and receive me among your people."

At this point the *yangona* root, an untidy mass of twigs, wrapped in newspaper, is pushed toward the chief. During the course of the little speech it has been pushed in his direction several times and then withdrawn as unworthy of being offered. This little ceremony was not performed by Stan himself, though he speaks Fijian well, but by his coxswain acting in the capacity of herald. Stan himself, as captain of a yacht, is a chief also.

At the end of the speech the *yangona* is received by the chief who says that it is a splendid and completely acceptable gift and that he welcomes the visitors and they will be under his protection for the time they are in his territory. This is no empty formula for the chief is the power in his village and means what he says. However poor the village, he will feed and entertain and house visitors he has received in this manner.

In the case of the village on Malolo, when the *yangona* was accepted, it was given to a man to be prepared as a drink which would be served to us all. We sat in the hut listening to the pounding outside as the root was prepared. When the *yangona* was brought in, it was contained not in a carved bowl but in an enamel washbasin. It was not served in the half coconut shell called a *bilo*, but in thick glasses.

This was the first time I had ever seen such a lack of tradition in a village, however poor. When we had drunk the *yangona* we went out to look around, glad to be out of the hut where the flies buzzed around our faces.

There were no men at work in the village other than the one we had seen fishing on the reef. The village work was being done by the children. A group of perhaps twenty of them were sitting on the beach, extracting the meat of the coconut from the shell to make copra. It was a sad and depressing sight and a taint of degeneracy seemed to lie over the whole village. But Malolo, in its day, made history for it was on Malolo that the first American naval officers were killed by Fijians. And it was on this island that the United States made its might terribly felt and taught a lesson that lasted for a long time in the memory of the islanders.

In the year 1840 Commodore Charles Wilkes led an exploring and surveying squadron of the United States Navy into the Fiji Islands. This was the same Commodore Wilkes who twenty-one years later brought Britain to the verge of war with the United States by stopping the British packet *Trent* on the high seas and taking off two agents of the Confederate southern states on their way to England. He was an excellent navigator and an explorer and surveyor second only to England's James Cook. His charts of the Fiji Islands were the first authentic charts produced and are still in use and reliable to this day.

Two of his ship's officers, Lieutenant Underwood and Midshipman Henry, who had gone ashore at Malolo to obtain food, had been clubbed and killed. This was the first time that such a thing had happened to Wilkes' men and it happened because Underwood, ignoring explicit instructions, had gone ashore without sufficient arms and the Fijians discovered this. The bodies were recovered and to prevent their being eaten were buried on a sand island some distance off.

Wilkes determined to avenge the deaths in such a manner that nothing of the sort would happen again. Even while the officers were being buried he had his ship's boats posted around

Malolo to prevent any of the Fijians escaping the vengeance that was to come. When the funeral was over the attack on the island began.

The French had avenged the death of a rascally captain by burning a town to the ground. The British had sent a warship to avenge the death of four British seamen but the culprits could not be named for certain, and on the advice of the missionaries the British captain contented himself with issuing a stern warning.

Wilkes believed these measures too soft and thought that a sterner lesson was needed if foreign ships were to be safe in the future.

On Malolo there were two villages, one on the north and the other on the south of the island. Men from both villages had been involved in the murder of the two officers. The names of the villages were Arro and Sualib. They were to be attacked by separate parties of the Americans and Wilkes himself led the attack on Arro.

The village had been abandoned but it was burned to the ground and the plantations around it destroyed. Meanwhile the other party, under Lieutenant Commander Ringgold, attacked Sualib. Here most of the warriors from Arro had gathered.

They believed Sualib to be impregnable for it had never been conquered despite many attacks by other Fijians. It was surrounded by a ditch twelve feet wide and full of mud and water. Beyond the ditch was a palisade of coconut trunks and a wickerwork fence about ten feet high. Inside the palisade was another ditch and the earth from it had been thrown up to form a breastwork behind which the defenders could hide from musket fire.

The people were so sure of their prowess that they charged out to meet the American party and loosed a flight of arrows at them. They were met with musket fire and rockets and fled inside the palisade. When they had got in and the great war gate had been shut, they shouted in their defiance, "*Lako-mai*," meaning, "Come on," and waved their clubs and spears at the Americans.

At seventy feet from the palisade, the Americans opened fire. To their astonishment the Fijians, who showed themselves on the top of the war fence, were able to dodge the bullets. As soon as they saw the flash of the musket, they ducked and did this so quickly that the balls sped over them. Even the Fiji women and children joined in the defense of their town, firing their arrows. There was a standoff for a quarter of an hour, after which the efforts of the defenders slackened.

A rocket fired into the village set alight the thatch of one of the roofs. The flames spread quickly and panic broke out. Still the Fijians kept firing. The Fijians had muskets but did not know how to aim them properly and had mistaken notions of how much powder to use. They believed the amount of powder depended on the size of the man they were going to shoot and so carefully looked their enemy over to decide how much powder to use in the musket. Many exploded as a result. The women and children used the bows and arrows.

The village was now ablaze and the heat was so intense that Ringgold drew his men off to a coconut grove to wait until the flames subsided. It took an hour for the village to burn down when the Americans entered. Four bodies were found inside, among them that of a child.

Meanwhile the ship's boats had been fighting canoes full of warriors. One boat with seven men captured four canoes with a total of thirty-two warriors aboard.

Most of the warriors who had escaped the village of Sualib fled to the mountaintops where they could be seen gathered on the peaks. Wilkes fired rockets at them and at the end of the day, not only had the two villages on the island been destroyed, but all the plantations around them also, as well as all the canoes of the islanders that could be found.

In the evening of this terrible day an old Fijian ventured down onto the beach with two others and by signs indicated that he wanted to talk to one of the American officers. An interpreter was found and the old man said that he was the chief of Arro. He was homeless now and had lost all his property. His son was killed and so were many of his people. He offered some pigs as compensation for the killing of the American officers and stated that he had nothing to do with this killing. He begged that no further punishment should be meted out to his people. He was sent away without any assurance that there would be no further retribution.

On the following day, the officers and their men, having returned to the boats during the night, saw a few natives on the beach. Wilkes had been hoping that during the night some further overture asking for peace would be made. He had not been present when the chief from Arro had asked for an end to hostilities. Hoping that these natives were peace emissaries he went ashore in his gig. As he approached the beach, however, the men fled but they left a young woman who had with her several articles of clothing belonging to Lieutenant Underwood and Midshipman Henry, the two who had been killed.

She held in her arms a white cock which she asked Wilkes to accept. But Wilkes refused it, believing it to be a token of peace. If he accepted the white cock all would be over and he wanted to effect an unconditional and public surrender, believing this was necessary to drive the message home and insure the safety of white men and their ships in future.

He knew enough of the people by this time to realize that unless an abject surrender of this sort was made, with the natives throwing themselves on the mercy of their enemies in public, they would not regard themselves as defeated. The girl pleaded for peace saying that her people were sorry for having attacked and killed the "little chiefs."

But Wilkes would have none of this. He sent two Fiji

126

youths, who had been captured, to the chieftains of the two towns stating his terms. These were that he would assemble with his officers and men on the top of a hill later that day. The people of the island, under their chiefs, were to meet him there in a body and beg for pardon and sue for mercy in the presence of the whole of Wilkes' squadron.

The messengers went off and Wilkes led his men to the top of the hill. "The day was perfectly serene," he wrote in the narrative of his stay in Fiji. "And the island which but a few hours before was one of the loveliest spots in creation was now entirely laid waste, showing the place of massacre, the ruined town, and the devastated plantations. The eye wandered over the dreary waste to the beautiful expanse of waters beyond and around with the long lines of white sparkling reefs until it rested far in the distance on the small green spot where we had performed the last rites to our murdered companions."

The islanders came at last to the appointed hill. The first sign of them was the sound of wailing which grew louder and louder and then the natives were seen coming out of their hiding places. When they reached the foot of the hill on which Wilkes and his men were assembled, they were in such fear that they would not come any further until they were assured that their petition would be received. When this assurance was given they came slowly up the hill and forty men, crouching on their hands and knees and moaning and wailing, crept toward the feet of the Americans.

They stopped some thirty feet off and an old man who was their leader begged for pardon and forgiveness and pledged in the name of all that they would never again harm a white man. He stated that he acknowledged his people had been conquered; that the island belonged to the conquerors; that they were their slaves; that they had lost everything; that the two great chiefs of the island and all their best warriors had been killed, all their provisions destroyed and their houses burned.

127

They said they had brought two of the chief's daughters as a present for Wilkes.

Wilkes wanted to know why his officers had been killed and was told that they were killed without any cause for they had not done any injury to anyone but that those who slayed them were now all dead. He gave the Fijians a very stern lecture, refused the gift of the two daughters, warned them that if there was any other aggression against the whites their punishment would be even more terrible, and then granted them pardon on condition that they did as he told them.

He then ordered them to assemble on the morrow, unarmed and bringing every article they could find that belonged to the murdered men, and then they would be employed without recompense in bringing water for the vessels of his squadron.

This was agreed to and the next day Wilkes' ships were watered by the islanders of Malolo who carried some three thousand gallons of water on board. (Some of them complained that the work was so hard they would sooner have been killed in the battle.) Despite the loss of their food, they brought twelve pigs for the ships, some yams and about three thousand coconuts.

Wilkes again lectured the chiefs, warning them against attacking any whites and they assured him that should any white men come to their island in future, they would treat them as their own children. Wilkes discovered that in the attack on the island fifty-seven of the Fijians had been killed without the loss of a single American.

When he returned to the United States, Wilkes was charged with cruel, merciless and tyrannical behavior toward the natives but though the matter came into court, he was acquitted. His vengeance was undoubtedly harsh but news of his action spread through the Fijis and although foreigners continued to be murdered and eaten on the islands for many years, it can

128

be firmly argued that many more might have suffered that fate but for the Malolo incident.

The whites most likely to be killed were the missionaries. In denouncing such practices as the strangling of wives, polygamy and cannibalism, they were flying directly in the face of terrible but cherished Fiji traditions and undermining the authority of the chiefs. And yet only one missionary was ever killed, the Reverend Thomas Baker who was clubbed in 1867. He was killed by an inland tribe, and the reason for his murder is still a mystery. The body was cut up, cooked and eaten, portions being sent to other tribes as gifts.

According to the story I heard, the Reverend Baker wore elastic-sided boots which were thought to be part of his feet and were cooked with them. Those who received the feet complained that they were uneatable.

Chapter Seventeen

BY the middle of the nineteenth century it was becoming evident to many Fijians, chief among them Thakombau, that the white man represented a far greater power than they had ever before encountered.

The Fijians were coming in contact with the white man's law and were impressed, though they did not understand it. They did not distinguish much between nationalities—American, British and French—but saw all white men as having the same law. That law was related to the white man's religion, Christianity. To ally themselves with the white man and obtain his protection and goodwill, it was plainly necessary to become Christian. But this put them in conflict with their own chiefs. The chiefs were nearer than the white men and though the missionaries did make many converts among the lower classes of Fijians, their hope of real success lay in the conversion of the chiefs themselves.

It was hard for a chief to become a Christian—hard for him to give up his many wives, his arbitrary powers of life and death, his ability to exact tribute, to go to war and to make peace. The old chief at Somosomo who had begged the missionaries to come to his land only to make things so unpleasant for them that they left, died a pagan. His son, the terrible Tui Kilakila, succeeded him. He was clubbed to death by his son while asleep. And the son, after a brief period of power, was murdered by his brother, and the great kingdom of Somosomo fell apart in fratricidal warfare so that it was soon in ruins, never to rise again.

Some of the chiefs, seeing the fate of Somosomo, gave a little more ear to the missionaries who pointed out, with truth, that had the old king and his people become Christians no such disaster would have overtaken his family and his people.

The attack on Malolo was not the only act of retribution performed by Commodore Wilkes while in Fiji. Captain Hudson, who was attached to Commodore Wilkes' squadron, was assigned to capture Vendovi, the man responsible for the attack on the American Bêche-de-Mer ship *Charles Doggett* eight years previously when ten men had been killed. Vendovi was captured and taken away with Wilkes' squadron to the United States and the Fijians never saw him again. That left a tremendous impression on them.

The missionaries in their work got plenty of support from the white men's warships with their big guns and in this state of affairs, some of the chieftains softened toward Christianity, while others toughened their attitude. Among the latter was Thakombau, now a giant of a man both physically and in his authority. Though his old father, Tanoa, was still alive and Thakombau acknowledged him as king, it was he who wielded the power in Mbau.

Thakombau early developed hostility toward Christianity. It was hostility more of attitude than of action. When the first missionaries came to Mbau they had been given a site on the crowded island in which to build a house. But Thakombau warned the missionary, the Reverend William Cross, that he was engaged in a war and wouldn't be able to think about religion for some time, nor would he be able to protect the mission. Since two chiefs had been eaten and two more were cooking when the Reverend Cross arrived, and the tiny island was seething with warriors in a war frenzy, he decided not to try to establish a mission there at that time. He, therefore, went to Rewa on the mainland where he was well received and started a mission.

But Rewa was the traditional enemy and the chief rival of

Mbau at this time. To Thakombau it looked as though the Christians, with all the power they had from their god, had gone over to his rival. When later a second attempt was made to establish a mission at Mbau, Thakombau refused permission because the Reverend Cross would not trust himself on the island on his first visit.

For years, then, Mbau remained not only the major Fiji power but also the fortress of the heathens. Thakombau did allow the missionaries to work at Rewa two miles away. He received the missionaries and listened to their talk but never showed any signs of conversion. When he was warned of the fires of hell into which he would be cast if he did not repent his sins, he said, "Ah, well, it is a good thing to have a hot fire in cold weather."

Pique against the Christians was undoubtedly a big factor in Thakombau's remaining a heathen and the champion of heathenism. But he also saw in Christianity a challenge—indeed a grave threat to the authority of the chiefs and the traditions of the Fijians. He sensed that times would change and were changing for he was a man of extraordinary intelligence. Yet he was determined to resist the change as long as he might.

In his early enmity toward the Christians, Thakombau liked to taunt them with their own doctrines. On one occasion when a tribe that had been Christianized was attacked by another, a greater tribe which was still pagan, the missionaries sent to Thakombau and asked him to intervene.

"I shall not protect them and I rejoice that you have now a fight of your own," replied the king. "When I ask you Christian people to help me in war, you say, 'No, it is not lawful for Christians to fight,' and here we are breaking our backs by steering our canoes, catching dysentery by sleeping aboard in the dews and rains, and being shot in great numbers while the Christians sit quietly at home all the time. Now you have a fight of your own and I am glad of it." He sent not a single warrior to aid the Christian tribe and rumor had it that Thakombau himself had instigated the war to see what kind of men the Christians were.

In 1843 a long-expected major war between Mbau and Rewa broke out. It was a war such as could only be fought in Fiji, complicated by blood ties and allegiances which crossed over the lines of conflict. There was a Rewa party at Mbau which was led by one Arivalita, who was halfbrother to Thakombau and his rival. Similarly there was a Mbau party at Rewa led by the brother of King Dreketi of Rewa—the same Phillips who had sailed on an American whaler and mixed up seaman slang in his English speaking. Both sides in the conflict assembled large armies but as was often the case in Fiji wars, the two armies never met. Instead they raided each other's territories, in commando-like attacks and in the first months of the war, Rewa was worsted, and its people driven back into its principal town. The war went on for ten years in a patchwork of plots, raids and assassinations but its chief result in the early stages was to put the weight of the Christians against Thakombau.

Thakombau, shortly before the end of the first stage of the war, had blockaded the island of Viwa where there was a large Christian community. He also ordered all the whites out of Levuka and they were not allowed to return there for several years. These two actions against the Christians produced an alliance between Christians and Rewans which was to prolong the war, and nearly ruin him.

Perhaps Thakombau sensed the size of the force that might be allied against him if the whites took sides against him when H.M.S. *Havanna* one of the ships in Victoria's navy, visited Ovalau in 1849. He then witnessed a demonstration of naval gunnery. A target was set up on a rock eight hundred yards distant and blown to pieces by the guns of the ship. Thakombau turned to a missionary who was present and said, "This makes me tremble. We are no longer safe. If we offend these people they will bring their ship to Mbau. They will

133

find us out with their spyglasses and they will destroy us and our town."

Actually a similar incident which was to make fear of the white man and his warships a reality had already occurred in Thakombau's domain. There was living in Fiji at the time a man, John Brown Williams, of Salem, Massachusettes. He had been formerly the United States Consul in New Zealand and was now the United States Commercial Agent for Fiji. He obtained permission to move to the islands in 1845 and settled a year later at the island of Nukulau where he was soon engaged in land speculation of the shadiest kind.

He and his partners, for he had several, bought the island of Nukulau off Suva for thirty dollars and Lauthala Point on the main island nearby for fifty dollars. He registered these deeds with himself and then made himself the sole proprietor by merely scratching out his partners' names on the deed.

Nukulau, a short distance off the coast from Suva, is a pretty little holiday island these days for the people in the capital of Fiji. Each weekend in the dry season there is a procession of launches, cruisers, and sailboats over to Nukulau for picnics. The island is low lying, can be walked around in half an hour, has pretty beaches, clear water and groves of coconut. It was on this island, bought for thirty dollars, that an incident took place that brought Thakombau face to face with the muzzles of the naval guns of the United States.

On the Fourth of July, 1849, Williams was celebrating Independence Day on Nukulau with salvos fired from cannons and muskets. One of the cannon exploded and Williams' house caught fire. There were a number of Fijians on the island from Mbengga and Rewa. Instead of helping to put out the fire, over which they rejoiced, they seized the opportunity to loot the house, carrying off anything they could lay hands on. This was a usual procedure, normally passed over, but Williams was not of the sort to pass it over. He declared that the United States Consulate had been looted by

Fijian cannibals and an indemnity must therefore be paid. Thakombau was the paramount chief and he, then, was the man who must pay the indemnity.

The indemnity asked was far beyond his means—five thousand dollars. The matter was referred for arbitration to the captain of a United States ship of war.

Chapter Eighteen

FROM the time of the restoration of his father, Tanoa, to the throne (if such it might be called) of Mbau, Thakombau had had one overriding ambition. It was to make himself not merely king of Mbau and its many dependencies but *Tui Viti*—King of Fiji.

No other chief in all the history of the islands ever held such an ambition or could ever think in terms of one central government for the islands. It was the genius of Thakombau that he alone could do so. His father still occupied the throne of Mbau and the son, unlike so many others, respected his father and did not plot against him for power. Nonetheless, Thakombau was the real power in his father's land. He well knew that the islands of Tonga were now ruled by one king —King George—who was his ally and was also at least nominally a Christian. He knew also that the Hawaiian Islands of which he had heard from the missionaries and ships' captains were also under control of a king. That he then should become King of Fiji seemed proper and alone would satisfy his ambition.

Despite his enmity toward Christians he would not allow their missionaries to be touched. He might provoke wars against Christian settlements but he would not himself go directly to war against them. He tried to straddle the fence dividing paganism from Christianity and undoubtedly reflected many times that Christianity had produced a king in Tonga and another in Hawaii. Paris might have been worth a Mass to one French king, but as yet Fiji was not worth a baptism to Thakombau.

King George of Tonga, however, had a real ship and so, Thakombau heard, had the King of Hawaii. Thakombau wanted one. He owned the finest canoes in the South Pacific and his own personal vessel *Ra Marama* was a hundred and two feet long, its twin hulls were six feet deep and it could not be called by so small a word as a canoe. It was indeed a splendid Fiji warship.

Yet its ownership did not carry the same prestige as would the ownership of one of the white men's vessels. Thakombau determined then to get one and an old Fiji hand, Captain Wallace of Salem, Massachusetts, was commissioned to have a brig built for Thakombau in America. Thakombau was to pay one thousand *piculs* of Bêche-de-Mer for the vessel.

Months went by and no brig appeared. A shipbuilder in Australia heard of Thakombau's ambition and offered him a large ketch. Like a little boy who could not wait for his birthday present, Thakombau agreed to accept the ketch for which he would pay five hundred *piculs* of Bêche-de-Mer. The ketch arrived and with it the seller, William Owen, who brought along a large brigantine also in which to carry away the five hundred *piculs* of Bêche-de-Mer.

Thakombau sent orders througout his dominions for collection of the "fish." The divers had hardly started working when the brig he had ordered from America arrived. With it came Captain Wallace in a large bark intent upon carrying off the thousand *piculs* promised in payment for the fine new ship appropriately named in bright gold lettering on its stern, Thakombau. Thakombau, then, had to collect one hundred tons of Bêche-de-Mer to pay for these two vessels—an impossible quantity when it is realized that each of the dried sea slugs weighed only a few ounces.

Thakombau had obtained about one hundred and thirty *piculs* of Bêche-de-Mer toward payment for the Australian ketch. He called the ketch deal off and asked for the value of the Bêche-de-Mer back in ammunition. He was told that the "fish" were forfeit because of the cancellation of the contract and now he had to collect the price of his wonderful new vessel from America.

He issued orders to the chiefs in whose districts the sea slugs were plentiful to start collecting them with greater energy. He sent bundles of sacks to the chiefs to put the dried Bêche-de-Mer in.

But the people and the chiefs grumbled at this levy, worked only grudgingly and in some parts refused to work at all. Thakombau sailed among the islands on a sort of royal picnic aboard his ship to find very little Bêche-de-Mer prepared in payment for it. In desperation he collected about twelve thousand fighting men, put them in eighty magnificent canoes, and took them to the Macuata coast off Viti Levu where the Bêche-de-Mer were plentiful in the warm shallow waters. The warriors were to force the people to collect the slugs and also help to collect them themselves.

This massive attempt was only partially successful. In the end Captain Wallace had to leave the ship with Thakombau, having received only about five hundred *piculs* of Bêche-de-Mer in payment.

But as matters turned out Thakombau had paid more for his ship than the five hundred *piculs*. He had paid heavily in prestige. His subject peoples had refused to obey his orders and had escaped punishment. And the white Bêche-de-Mer traders were angry at this invasion of their business by so powerful a chief. They joined the Rewa discontents under Quaranqio and the Christians in a loose but growing federation against Thakombau.

Then came the crisis which the missionaries had long feared. Thakombau's aged father died. His death had been long expected and the missionaries had pleaded with Thakombau not to strangle the old king's wives so that their spirits could accompany him on his journey through the next world as was the custom. Captains of English and American ships of war had also warned Thakombau against following this practice. The missionaries rightly saw that if the custom were not observed on the death of so powerful a king, then the strangling of widows would decline. Even before Tanoa died the missionaries offered ten whale's teeth weighing twenty pounds—an enormous treasure—if the wives were spared, and the Reverend Calvert even offered to follow the Fiji custom of mourning for the dead king by amputating one of his fingers if the wives were spared. But no promise was given by Thakombau.

As Tanoa lay dying the missionaries again pleaded with Thakombau but he would yield nothing. He sensed that they were right, and that the wives should not be strangled. Yet he was faced with a crisis of custom. He was about to become the most powerful King of Fiji. He would rule over lesser kings to whom the strangling of the widows was a sacred matter. If he satisfied the Christians he would outrage many of his subjects. If he satisfied his subjects and honored his father in the traditional way, he would outrage the Christians. He listened to the missionaries in an agony of indecision.

One of his chiefs who reproved the missionaries for interfering was himself reproved by Thakombau. "The missionaries are right," cried the king. "Please, sirs, continue with your efforts." He sent missionaries to see the wives who would be killed. The missionaries saw them and each one was quite resolved to be strangled. One missionary warned the women that if they permitted themselves to be killed, they would burn eternally in the fires of hell. "Who fears hell?" cried one woman. "We shall jump in there the day our king dies."

Tanoa died during the night of December 8, 1852. The Reverend Watsford, who had been principal among the missionaries pleading for the lives of the condemned women, arrived at Mbau early on the morning of the ninth and saw six biers standing outside the door of the dead king. He knew then that five wives were to be killed, the sixth bier being for the king himself.

He went in to find the murders had already started. One woman was dead. Another had the cord around her neck. As the missionary stood in the doorway she collapsed to the floor dead. The third was now summoned and Thakombau spotted the missionary and cried to him, "What about it, Mr. Watsford?"

"Refrain, sir. That is plenty. Two are dead. Refrain—I love them," cried Mr. Watsford.

"We also love them," replied Thakombau. "They are not many—only five. But for you missionaries many more would have been strangled for my father." The stranglings went on in the presence of the missionary until five had been killed. Thakombau, himself in an agony of mind, had to assist with the strangling of his own mother, and the missionary continued to plead for the life of each woman until she was dead. Immediately afterwards Thakombau was formally proclaimed Vanivalu—"The Root of War" and King of Mbau.

Shortly after his proclamation as King of Mbau and indeed, as *Tui Viti* or King of Fiji, Thakombau's fortunes ebbed. The war with Rewa flared up anew, this time with the whites against him. They armed, defied him, and eventually, entering into a league with his enemies. They established a blockade of Mbau. No ship was allowed to approach the little island. Its food and supplies of ammunition upon which Thakombau depended were cut off.

To add to his troubles Thakombau's fortress of Kaba at the mouth of the Rewa River, held by five hundred of his own men, rebelled. In the fortress were the sails of Thakombau's brig. He was left with a ship for which he had paid heavily in prestige but which, without sails, could not be moved from its anchorage. Thakombau led an attack on Kaba. He was defeated and his prestige fell to its lowest ebb. No man would lift a hand to help him and there were daily plots against his life.

When things were at their worst, King George of Tonga, on his way to Sydney, Australia, visited Thakombau. He listened to his story, sympathized with him, and made the offhand remark that the Kaba fortress did not seem to him impregnable. Thakombau sensed in this a hint of help and promised to give King George his great canoe *Ra Marama* —"The Great Lady"—on his return. King George of Tonga had one word of advice for Thakombau: that he should become a Christian. But Thakombau was not yet ready.

More disasters followed. A fire broke out in Mbau destroying much of the town and was followed by a hurricane. An attack on Kaba failed utterly. Williams published a letter in the Australian newspapers calling on the civilized nations of the world to destroy that "Sink of iniquity Mbau which," he added, "a warship might easily do while one is smoking a cigar."

The people of Mbau, Williams said, were guilty of every kind of savagery and should be swept from the face of the earth. Thakombau's friend, King George of Tonga, sent this newspaper clipping to him and with it he enclosed a letter which said, "I expect to visit you with the Tongan friends to bring away my canoe; and when we have finished planting we shall come to you."

There was an influence of help here in the phrase "Tongan friends," for the Tongans, under one of their chiefs, Ma'afa, were now the best organized fighting force in Fiji and had made themselves very largely the masters of the eastern Fiji Islands. But they were Christians and could not be expected to fight on behalf of so proclaimed a pagan as Thakombau.

King George's letter concluded by urging Thakombau again to become a Christian and to be humble. "It will be well for you, Thakombau, to think wisely in these days," King George wrote.

Thakombau thought the letter over for three days and then sent for the Reverend J. Waterhouse. It was not easy for such a man as he to desert the gods of his fathers and accept a new religion. He talked for a long time with the Reverend Waterhouse and then called a meeting of those few remaining chiefs who would answer his summons. He told them that he had decided to *lotu*—to become a Christian. Many demurred, but Thakombau remained firm. On Sunday, April 30, 1854, dressed in his finest robes, he called his people together and publicly renounced the gods of his fathers and stated he had decided to become a Christian.

He ordered the pagan temples destroyed. He ordered a magnificent grove of casuarina trees, sacred to the old gods, cut down. He proclaimed that cannibalism and the strangling of widows was to cease and he gave his permission to his people to attend the mission houses and become Christians. They flocked to them, begging, not so much for Christianity, as to be taught to read. They had a thirst for learning.

Christianity did not bring an end to Thakombau's troubles. Rather his conversion brought new disasters. His enemies among the whites regarded his conversion as a mere subterfuge and became more suspicious and hostile. Chiefs and tribes who had remained loyal to him as the defender of paganism revolted. Whole areas went over to his enemies. Towns within a mile or two of Mbau now dared to place themselves under the protection of the enemies of Mbau and within Mbau itself there were plots as thick and as tangled as jungle growth.

Two of Thakombau's younger brothers went over to the rebels and the tiny island was plunged into a state of seige. Then Thakombau fell ill. His body was covered with sores and he trembled with fever. There is room for the suspicion that his food was being tampered with. Certainly there were enough who heartily wished him dead. Even the Reverend

Calvert who had worked hard for his conversion proposed to Thakombau that he fly from his island and seek refuge somewhere else.

Thakombau's reply was magnificent. "If evil comes, I must die," he replied. "I cannot run away from it."

The island of Mbau was now paralyzed by the blockade of both whites and Fijians. Then the American ship *Dragon* arrived at Levuka with supplies. The captain, Thomas C. Dunn, learned of the state to which Thakombau had come and although he was threatened by the merchants of Levuka, he ran their blockade and dropped his anchor off the island and brought supplies ashore.

From that day forward Captain Dunn proved a friend to Thakombau. The breaking of the blockade saved him and proved the turning of the tide for him. The chiefs of Rewa fell out among themselves and the threat to Mbau from that quarter failed. The people wanted peace and so did Thakombau. The war was ended on February 9, 1855.

After the peace with Rewa there remained of the war only the rebellion of the Mbau warriors at Kaba who had stolen the sails of Thakombau's now useless ship. They were led by one Mara who proclaimed that there could be no peace until Thakombau was dead.

Mara now became the champion of the heathens and the war took on a new twist—Christianity versus heathenism with Thakombau, surprisingly, the champion of the Christians. He wisely waited before attacking Kaba for the promised help from Tonga. King George himself was coming with a fleet of thirty canoes. He intended to act as a mediator and not to fight but his hand was forced for one of his chiefs was killed by musket-shot fired by one of Mara's men. The death of the Tongan had to be revenged.

A mixed army of Fijians and Tongans moved to attack Kaba. At the first assault the defenders oppened fire and a number of Fijians were killed. According to the rules of

Fijian warfare the battle was lost for whoever suffered the first heavy blow was reckoned defeated.

But the Tongans either had not heard of these rules or decided to ignore them. They charged on in a frenzy, poured over the barricades leaving a trail of wounded and dead behind them, and took the town.

Kaba had fallen; the rebellion against Thakombau was ended. But the victory belonged to the Tongans and neither they nor Thakombau could ever forget that.

Chapter Nineteen

AFTER the peace with Rewa, Thakombau hoped that he had reached the end of his troubles. He was firmly back on his throne and his enemies had been conquered and dispersed.

Now a Christian, he gave some proof of the depth of his conversion by pardoning his enemies instead of clubbing them. But he had forgotten about one petty event which was to change the whole future of Fiji. He had forgotten about the burning of the rascally United States Agent Williams' house on Nukulau and the five thousand dollars that Williams claimed as compensation for looted property.

Williams drew up a list of the articles which he insisted had been stolen. As an agent of the United States government, he pressed for action from Washington. An American warship the USS *St. Mary,* visited Fiji in 1851 and Williams presented his claim for compensation to the captain. But the captain was not able to complete an investigation and left the matter in the hands of the Reverend James Calvert and David Whippy. These two were instructed to report their findings to the commander of the next American war vessel to visit Fiji.

Then another house of Williams' was burned down, this time by the people of Rewa following the death of their chief Qaraniqio. Six months later, in September 1855, Commander E. B. Boutwell arrived on the warship *John Adams.* Williams was soon on board complaining of his losses. An investigation was held without Thakombau being present and without Whippy or the Reverend Calvert being consulted. Boutwell administered a rough brand of quarterdeck justice and decided that Thakombau should pay an indemnity, not of five thousand dollars, but thirty thousand dollars.

The American Captain insisted that since Thakombau claimed to be king of Fiji he alone was responsible for any property losses incurred by American citizens in the islands. Boutwell was cautioned by a senior captain of another vessel which arrived at the time, "to adhere strictly to his instructions." Boutwell's reaction was to reopen the case and the indemnity demanded of Thakombau was once again raised, this time to $43,531.

Thakombau was summoned on board the American ship, a paper was put before him and Williams told him to sign it. He refused. In a rage Captain Boutwell said, "You must sign it or I will take you away to America." Remembering the fate of a Fijian warrior who was carried off by Commodore Wilkes never to be seen again in Fiji, and the appalling demonstration of naval gunnery given by the British warship, Thakombau signed.

He soon came to his senses, however, and realized that he had committed himself to pay this huge sum of money within a period of two years and if he did not do so, he would have to resign the government of Mbau and would be taken for punishment to America on the first warship that called after the expiration of that period. He consulted with the missionaries who wrote a protest for him which was forwarded to the United States Consul at Sydney. There was no reply.

Three years later the United States corvette *Vandalia*, under Captain Sinclair, arrived in the Fijis with a double mission. The first part was to avenge an attack on a boat's crew in which the crew had been killed and eaten, one of them being an American. This occurred in the northwestern group of islands, the Yasawas. Fifty men from the *Vandalia* attacked the island responsible. They faced five hundred warriors, killed twenty of them, and had five of their number wounded.

The second part of Captain Sinclair's mission was to collect the money from Thakombau. Thakombau was summoned on board and told, according to his own report, that he must pay, "either in cash or in blood." Once more he was threatened and once more, under threats, forced to sign a document which he could not read. This document turned out to be a promise to pay forty-five thousand dollars in one year—presumably the original amount plus accumulated interest.

Such a payment was far beyond his ability, and horribly out of proportion to the damage done to Williams' property.

A little while before Britain had appointed a consul, William Thomas Pritchard, to the islands and, threatened by the United States because of the Fourth of July fire to Williams' house, Thakombau turned now to Pritchard. He proposed that Britain annex the Fiji Islands subject to a few conditions, one of which was that Britain would pay Thakombau's debt to the United States.

As soon as he had this request in writing Pritchard left for Sydney on his way to London to ask the Gladstone government to accept the offer. He had actually been only eight weeks in Fiji but in that time he had put into effect a system of consular courts in which white traders and Fijians could plead their cases and had won the confidence of all who knew him.

But he had made a few mistakes. He had accepted Thakombau's claim to be King of Fiji and this was, in truth, an ambition rather than a reality. The Tongans, under Ma'afu, were now prominent in the eastern island and had seized the southern islands of Matuku and Totoya. They were the only disciplined army in Fiji and though their behavior in war was outrageous, they were always able to justify their actions by claiming that they were merely protecting their own Tongan missionaries and teachers.

The white missionaries denounced their excesses which at times included the flogging of Fijian chiefs to exact tribute. The missionaries even went so far as to expell Ma'afu from the church. But he ignored this expulsion, and, posing as the cultured Tongan Christian, went on with his murderous raids. Added to the Tongan claims to sovereignity over some of the Fiji Islands there were other chiefs who did not acknowledge Thakombau as the sovereign.

So Pritchard went to London with an offer of cession from a man who was not in a position to make such an offer. The offer was received with interest, however, for the British government was becoming disturbed over French and American influence in the Fijis. Pritchard was sent back to Fiji to be there when the Americans once more pressed their claim against Thakombau.

In his absence, however, Ma'afu, by insinuating himself into Fijian quarrels, had become master of half the islands in the group and Thakombau did not have the forces to challenge him directly. When Pritchard came back Thakombau protested to him that the Tongan's conquests were actually an attack on Britain herself since he had ceded the islands to Great Britain. Ma'afu also saw Pritchard and calling Thakombau "an old savage" proposed that Pritchard support the Tongans when he, as their leader, would hand the islands over to Britain provided he continued to rule as king under the British government.

Pritchard called a meeting of all the chiefs including Thakombau and Ma'afu. He solved the difficulty with one stroke. He got Ma'afu to renounce all political claims in Fiji and all claims to lands that he had conquered. He got the chiefs to acknowledge Thakombau as their sovereign. He then received from Thakombau a new offer of cession going into considerable detail and this offer was signed by Thakombau, by Ma'afu and the principal chiefs of Vanua Levu and Lau.

Unfortunately for Pritchard he was more brilliant than his government. In London, the foreign minister, who was then the Duke of Newcastle, decided to send out another emissary to investigate and picked Colonel W. T. Smythe, a dull, unimaginative man for the task.

When Smythe turned in his report it was heavily loaded against British annexation of Fiji. He was an artillery officer rather than a diplomat and fitted that curious vein of British administrative thinking which had once put a cavalry officer in charge of the Royal Navy. Wherever he went, Smythe wore the plumes and braid of the full dress uniform of an officer of the Royal Artillery. His inquiries were not deep and his view was narrow. He relied heavily on hearsay, concluded that Thakombau was merely one of many chiefs in Fiji and had no claim to some two hundred thousand acres of land which Thakombau had offered to surrender to the British government.

He stated that Fiji was very difficult to reach and its navigation full of hazards from reefs and hurricanes. In short, Fiji was not required for the safety of Britain in the Pacific and in the event of war could hardly be defended. His report, when it reached London, was accepted. The offer of cession was declined and Pritchard, discredited, returned to London whence, despairing at the lack of vision in his own government, he went to the American West where he was killed by Indians.

As soon as the offer of cession had been turned down, Ma'afu, ignoring all that he had signed, again began his attacks behind the scenes on Thakombau. He made a claim against him, allegedly on behalf of King George of Tonga, for sixty thousand dollars. This was a great blow to Thakombau for King George of Tonga not only had taken Thakombau's beautiful canoe *Ra Marama* but had also taken his fine ship as well. After making the claim Ma'afu assembled a fleet at Rewa for an attack on Mbengga. But this came to nothing.

Then again came the terrible threat of the white men's ships. Father Breheret, head of the Roman Catholic Mission in Fiji, complained to the captain of the French corvette *Cornelie* that a Tongan chief had flogged Roman Catholic converts on the Yasawas. This flogging was, in part, a portion of Ma'afu's plan to bring the western Yasawa Island under his control. But through the years, there has been a hint of religious warfare in the matter. The Tongans were Wesleyans and a narrow bitterness had developed between Catholic and Wesleyan missionaries.

Pritchard, who had not yet left Fiji, investigated the incident and saw for himself the wounds on the back of the men who had been flogged. Captain Leveque of the *Cornelie* summoned Thakombau to his ship and directed that the Tongan chief be brought for punishment. Since he claimed to be the King of Fiji the responsibility for the flogging was laid at his door and he was kept a hostage on board for several weeks until the Tongan, Semisi, was produced. Semisi was tried, found guilty and sentenced to deportation and hard labor in the French settlements on New Caledonia. The *Cornelie* sailed with Semisi on board and nothing more was seen or heard of him in Fiji.

Here again was a terrible example of the white men's power and Thakombau trembled lest he suffer the same fate if he did not pay off Williams' claim. Williams died, however, and Thakombau breathed a little easier for he did not realize that Williams' claims had been turned into a claim, not by an individual, but by the United States government. Another American ship turned up, the USS *Tuscarora*, and again Thakombau was hauled on board and settlement of the Fourth of July fire and other claims demanded.

That Thakombau was incapable of meeting the demands scarcely troubled the American skippers. He was forced again to sign an agreement to pay the claim, this time in four yearly installments. When he hesitated, Captain Stanley threatened to use the ship's guns. Thakombau signed, and pledged as security three islands—Nairai, Mbatiki and Moturiki.

He was desperate now. In the face of the white men with their warships, power to decide the future of his people was slipping from his hands. His plea to be annexed by Britain had been turned down. He formed a government of his own over all his territories with an eye to establishing his position as King of Fiji. He had himself crowned with a crown made of zinc and studded with semiprecious stones. Surely the gold crown of England would accept and protect the zinc crown of Fiji, he argued.

But England would not. Eventually the United States Vice-Consul, who had succeeded Williams, suggested to Thakombau a way out. In brief it was that he should offer the two hundred thousand acres of land previously offered to Britain to a company of businessmen in Australia. These in return would pay off the American debt but they were also to receive wide trading and banking right in Fiji. In short, they were buying two hundred thousand acres of land and the economic future of Fiji for a little over forty thousand dollars.

A company was formed, a charter drawn up, but it was so unfair that the British Consul, John Bates Thurston, protested it and the matter was held over until a British ship, HMS *Challenger*, arrived. The captain of the *Challenger*, together with Thurston, had the charter rewritten and when this was done, it was signed by Thakombau. He was relieved of his debts but he had sold his birthright and indeed the birthright of many others. There was no other way out for him.

But he had one friend, Captain Thomas C. Dunn, who had lifted the blockade against him, and had written a letter to the *New York Herald* denouncing the whole shabby business of the American debt, asserting that Thakombau had been unjustly treated and time and again terrorized by ship's guns into signing iniquitous agreements to pay the damages.

The letter caused a public furor in the United States and the whole matter was reopened by the American government. Another American ship arrived in Fiji, the USS *Jamestown*, under Captain Truxton. Another inquiry was made and Williams' claims against Thakombau were disallowed.

The investigation had come too late, however. The Australian company known as the Polynesia Company had taken over Thakombau's debts. The company failed and the whole business passed away. It had had one deeply significant effect, and that was to plant in Thakombau's mind the need to obtain protection for his people from Britain—a curious result indeed of an American Independence Day celebration.

Chapter Twenty

AT the height of their power the Tongan stronghold was in the Eastern or Lau Group of the Fiji Islands. These islands, strung out in an arc running roughly from northwest to south, are a little over halfway from Tonga to Viti Levu, the great island of Fiji. It was here that the Tongans first came to have canoes built. Their own islands supplied no great stands of timber for canoes and the Fiji double-hulled vessel, called a *drua*, was far superior to their own. The hulls of the canoes were built in the Lau Group. But the Tongans obtained the mat sails from the Yasawas far away to the west. There the quality of the mats is superior to any produced in the Fijis. The building of a canoe called for purchases from both extremities of the Fiji group.

One of the principal islands on which canoes were built was Kambara. Indeed the last war canoe launched in the South Pacific was built there only a few years back and is there to this day. It is a half-sized vessel of not quite fifty feet. It was built for the use of a missionary who had no other method of getting around among the islanders.

Stan Brown told me the story of the building. The trade of canoe builder was passed on from family to family and its secrets preserved as family secrets. When the islanders decided to build a canoe for the missionary there was only one man living in Kambara who knew how to do the work. He had himself never built a canoe but his father had taught him every detail and he had committed the whole plan to memory. He was put in charge of the project and strictly observed all the ritual.

In the Clyde shipyards of Britain it is well known that no major work would be done on a ship on a Friday—the day of the crucifixion of Christ. There are similar days on which no work must be done on a Fiji war canoe and in the building of the Kambara canoe these days were strictly observed. Not a nail was used in putting the canoe together or a piece of manila rope for its lashings. The rope needed was sinnet, braided out of the fibers of the coconut, and where glue was required, it was prepared in the old way from the gum of trees.

When a canoe was to be launched in the old days many people were slaughtered and their bodies used as rollers over which to launch the vessel. The canoe was always built half a mile or more from the sea to prevent its being seized or burned by enemies. The Kambara canoe was also built half a mile inland. There was no road or trace leading from the canoe to the ocean and no tractor on the island which could tow the heavy vessel overland to the water. Stan wondered whether a mistake had not been made and whether the canoe, when complete, would be impossible to launch.

"The Fijians seem to have inherited memory of how things were done which constantly surprises me," Stan said. "I asked the *masai* or craftsman in charge of the canoe building where he, a Christian, was going to get the bodies to roll his canoe over down to the water. He replied that he would manage. The ceremonies of the presentation of the canoe were tremendously impressive. There was no money exchanged. The canoe builder was presented with yards of *tapa* and various gifts of this kind were given to all who had helped him build it.

"The canoe was to be launched at eleven o'clock in the morning when the tide would be right. At ten o'clock the ceremonies were still going on. At ten-fifteen nobody seemed to be in the slightest bit worried about launching the canoe

154

which was still half a mile from the sea and at ten-thirty I had concluded that it would not be launched that day.

"Then the launching started.

"The *masai* gave a few orders, men started climbing coconut palms with cutlasses and cutting off the fronds. In a matter of a few minutes they had lined the whole route from the canoe to the edge of the water with the fronds with the central stalk, which runs along the back, turned upwards. There was a shout, a few men seized poles, and levered the canoe onto the first of the palm branches and from there it slid all the way to the sea on the slippery palm fronds in a matter of minutes. A European contractor using a bulldozer and a trailer would have taken half a day and charged several hundred dollars."

When the canoe hit the water it floated exactly level, although, as noted, the man who built it had never built one before. The mast was raised, the ceremony of clubbing a few people and washing its decks with blood was omitted, and the canoe taken for a sail. I have heard that with a mat sail it registered twenty knots.

Kambara is a beautiful island. I reached it in the *Maroro* with Stan and was witness to the touching formality of requesting permission of the chief to land on his island. He received us in a magnificent mansion rather than hut of thatch. The posts supporting the roof and the rafters of the roof were strong and polished by the years and decorated with braided sinnet wrapped around them in a pattern.

The building was about thirty by sixty feet, cool and airy, and the whole floor covered with a silken handmade mat of pandanus. The mat was cushioned and, exceeding the liberties permitted a guest, I surreptitiously lifted it at one corner and found several mats below. I should think that we were sitting on three years' weaving by half a dozen people in the Yasawas where the mats had come from.

There was only one item of furniture in the lovely building which had several paneless windows opened to the sparkling sea. That was a straight-backed armchair of Victorian vintage. In this the chief sat and since none is allowed by custom to stand higher than the chief, we squatted on the floor, our legs akimbo (if the term may be applied to legs), and somewhat uncomfortable. White men's pelvic joints do not take readily to this position. Indeed, after my visit to the Fijis, when I sat in such a fashion for long periods on several occasions, I had for some months an aching in my joints that still returns occasionally.

Stan, through the medium of his Fijian coxswain, who had dressed himself in his best clothes for the occasion, presented his bundle of *yangona* roots with the usual little speech that the gift was utterly unworthy of the person to whom it was offered who would perhaps accept it only out of the generosity of his heart. Stan always uses a Fijian in these ceremonies although he is facile in the language. That is because it is proper to speak to a chief on a formal occasion through a minister or an ambassador.

When the *yangona* roots had been accepted a huge bowl of the drink was prepared and we were each given a half coconut shell to drink. Men were served first and the ladies afterwards but the first to drink was the chief himself.

The huge chief's house was cool and shaded. One of its most appealing features was the absence of furniture, and the consequent ease with which the house could be cleaned. A brush made of twigs from the coconut was all that was required to sweep the mat. And when the mat was swept the place was as clean as a pin.

Kambara is noted for its *tanoa* bowls. These are the huge, wooden, multilegged bowls carved out of a single block of wood in which *yangona* is served. They are carved with hand tools and in the old days these tools were adzes made of flint. There are no lathes to turn them on and no instruments to measure the sizes of the legs and see that they are all the same. But the people of Kambara produce their bowls in perfect symmetry, working only by eye. The bowls sell in the better decorators' stores of the United States for fifty dollars and up as centerpieces in which to put fruit. The people of Kambara sell them in faraway Suva for fifteen dollars.

After we had drunk our *yangona* Stan explained that we would like to buy a few articles from the people. The chief, a huge man in his sixties with a magnificent bush of iron-gray hair, inquired what articles we were interested in. We said bowls, shells and *tapa* or anything else produced on the island. He nodded gravely and replied that we should come to his dwelling at six that evening and he would tell the islanders to bring whatever they wished to sell to us there. Meanwhile we were free to go wherever we wished under his protection and he would appoint a man to accompany us who spoke a little English.

We left then to explore the village. It was almost pure Tongan, this having been, as noted, the stronghold of the Tongan invaders. The dwellings were walled in wickerwork panels framed with hibiscus wood. Each panel had a pleasing pattern of line rather than color worked into it—like the pattern in a tiled floor. The Fiji houses have a heavy look under their tremendous thatched roofs and with their walls of rough-looking pandanus leaves. From far off they resemble haystacks.

Compared with them the Tongan dwellings are airy and gay. The same is true of the Tongan *tapa* or cloth made from the bark of the paper mulberry. It is beaten out much finer and the design is usually black on white and therefore crisp and pleasing. Fiji *tapa*, which is called *masi*, employs two colors, black and a rich red-brown, which gives a heavy masculine look to the design it is laid against the white of the cloth itself.

In the village some women were employed making the paper cloth. They had a fibrous damp pulp laid upon a kind of trencher which they beat vigorously with little wooden clubs. As they beat, the pulp spread out thinner and thinner as pastry dough does when it is rolled. When a break appeared under the blows they folded the fibers back over it and mended the break by beating.

None could speak any English but they were full of fun and, seeing me staring at them, one moved over and handed me the mallet indicating that I should try to make the *tapa* too. I tried but with the first blow knocked a hole in the fabric and I was pushed out of the hut in a cascade of giggles.

The design which is put on the *tapa* is cut out of a stencil made from a banana leaf. There are some traditional designs but each worker makes a few variations of his own and so each piece of *tapa* is a creation in itself. The dyes used in the designs are made from lampblack mixed with coconut oil and a reddish earth, somewhat warmer than the painter's burnt sienna.

It is a labor of days to hand-paint with these dyes a piece of *tapa* eight feet long and two feet wide. But the people must take some pleasure in making the paper cloth. They wear it now only on formal occasions and yet still produce it, though the cheap T-shirts and other clothing of India are readily available to them.

I went toward the sea through a stately grove of coconuts in which little pigs grunted while searching for husks and the golden sunlight made a pleasing pattern of the fronds on the gleaming coral sand. A group of young girls clad in *sulus* and dripping wet came toward us carrying baskets made from fronds of the coconut. The baskets were full of fish, some of them still kicking.

The girls had been fishing off the reef and were happy at the thought of being able to tease us by frightening us with their fish. They produced lobsters and toothed parrot fish, watching us closely to see our reaction, and then one girl dipped into the bottom of her basket and giggling, produced a sizable octopus.

158

She was full of mischief, this one, and tried to pretend that the octopus had given her an fearsome fight and might, if she let it, strangle me. The girls were all Tonga-Fijians. Their skin was of the shade of almonds, their cheekbones pronounced and their hair straight and sable-dark. It hung to their waists, dripping with seawater, and there were little globules of water all over their skin, flashing in the sunlight.

They loved to giggle and tease and the one with the octopus indicated that she would like a cigarette. I gave her one and she took a mocking puff at it like a twelve-year-old showing how grown up she had become, and then passed it on to her companions who each took their puff, chattering away, with many asides among themselves, the substance of which I was to discover later.

I asked them how they fished and our interpreter who had a thorough command of kindergarten English explained that they dive down, trailing behind them a short line with a glittering unbaited hook at the end. That was all their equipment. They were magnificent swimmers, could stay underwater for two or three minutes, and by jerking the hook as they swam along lured the fish to strike.

They wore little plastic goggles to help them see underwater. How about sharks, for the reefs I knew were thick with them. They paid no attention to *qui*—their word for shark. If a shark came for them, they surfaced and did exactly what divers in America are told not to do—made a great deal of splash. The shark then went away. This tended to confirm my theory that sharks are regional in their behavior and what will excite them to attack in one area frightens them off in another.

Stan wanted us to see a Fiji fort on a mountaintop at one end of the island. He had done some investigation in the area and found several old Fiji arrowheads and speartips and was very excited about the place.

Stan assured us the fort was not far off and so we set out

for it. One of the characteristics of Englishmen is that they are not only great walkers but they are also fast walkers. An Englishman strolls at five miles an hour and when Stan led us off to see the fort, he was soon out of sight, leaving me jog-trotting along through the coconuts and pandanus trying to catch him.

The fort lay at the top of a rise of perhaps eight hundred feet. The approach to it was steep and tortuous. The entrance was through a rugged wall, partly natural rock and partly man-built. There was nothing there but the breast-high wall on the peak and the precipitous, twisting path below. And yet here was the mute testimnoy of the struggle between Fijian and Fijian, and between Fijian and Tongan. The place would be difficult to take even in our times. It might be bombed from the air but one defender could defy twenty trying to scale the precipice before it.

Standing in the fort I got for one moment a whiff of the fearsome dark wars between the Fijians and the Tongans. Far below us the dark growth of the island plunged down to the sparkling sea. A mile out lay the reef, a silvered slash in the sapphire ocean. Beyond lay other islands, bluer lumps in the blue. Through the ages a lookout had stood here with a signal drum beside him watching for canoes coming from these islands that might mean a feast or might mean a bloody slaughter resulting in a grim feast of the dead. The day was hot and the sun struck down around us but in this bloody place I felt chilled.

We went back down, more by the grace of God than any athletic ability of our own, and when we reached the coast trail leading to the fort, I said I would be hanged if I would walk back at the pace at which I had come.

This brought looks of amazement from Stan and two New Zealanders, who had accompanied me. They hadn't thought that we had been walking fast at all and spoke of visiting some other ruin which lay only an Englishman's mile off. But

160

Stan took pity on me. A party of Fijians were cutting coconut fronds to erect a temporary building in the village. The fronds were going to be taken on an outrigger down the coast and Stan said I could ride on the outrigger. And so I did. It was an enchanting journey.

I sat on a huge pile of slippery branches on the little canoe and was polled over the crystal waters down the coast to the village. The Fijians working the canoe could not speak English but laughed all the way and challenged another outrigger to a race. It was delightful to hear the tinkling of the hull against the wavelets, to see the splendid coral, as ornate as a wedding cake, slip by below us and feel the warm sea breeze on our faces. We were making, I would judge, a good six miles an hour in the light outrigger with the current behind us and the distance back to the village was about the same by sea as by land. As our outrigger pulled to the beach, Stan and the New Zealanders stepped out of the bush. Relieved of my presence, they had been able to stroll back at six miles an hour.

At six o'clock that evening we went to the chief's dwelling to see what was available for purchase. Word had been sent through the village that we wanted to buy some things. I am sure that in other parts of the world, we would have been plagued all day by people offering to sell us stuff. But we were the guests of the chief. He had given his orders and we were not once approached to buy anything at all.

The chief sat in his straight-backed armchair in the center of one wall of the hut and we were seated on his left side. The villagers were lined up on the floor with their goods before them on his right. We soon discovered that he was there in the position of a judge to see that we, his guests, were not charged too highly and that his people at the same time received a fair price for their goods.

The method of buying was very simple. A *tanoa* bowl was pushed forward toward us. It was a beautiful piece of work carved in the symbol of a turtle. That is to say it had the fins and head of the turtle strongly suggested with clean cuts of the wood but without any details.

"Five pounds," said the seller, holding up the fingers and thumb of one hand. I glanced at the chief. He shook his head.

"Three pounds," I replied. The seller drew the bowl back. I compromised on four pounds. The seller looked at the chief who nodded and the bowl was mine. So it went on. We bought *tapa*, both of Fiji and Tongan design and a number of shells, doing our best to convert Fiji pounds into American dollars.

There was a terrible shortage of change on the island and I had little with me. I found myself trying to convert Fiji shillings into American cents expressed in cowrie shells. The shells were valued at about a nickel apiece. They were of the common leopard cowrie but beautifully polished and cleaned. And so between shillings and nickels and shells and packets of cigarettes and a lot of laughter we bought mats and fans and *tapa* and *tanoa* bowls, and when we were done the chief signaled to the sellers that the market was closed and Stan's coxswain, or perhaps I should say his ambassador, picked up our purchases to take them to the *Maroro*.

That evening we learned that there was to be a *meke* or dance in the village, to which we were invited. We had gone ashore during the day in slacks and loose shirts but Stan intimated that we should dress more formally for the *meke*. It took place in a huge hut built for the occasion which was the reason the Fijians had been cutting the coconut fronds. A brand-new hut for a feast or a dance is not uncommon in Fiji.

We were seated at one end, having first removed our shoes out of care for the lovely pandanus matting on the floor. Off to one side, to our surprise, were a number of men playing cards with great gusto. They slapped the cards down on the pile as if they were war clubs, and smoked furiously while

162

they did it. Illumination was provided by hurricane lanterns slung on the upright poles of the hut. At the far end was the band—there was a guitarist, two or three players with large ukuleles and some magnificent drums hollowed out of the trunks of trees.

These ranged from one huge drum with a note like thunder to smaller drums held across the knees and which, when beaten with sticks, sounded like castanets. Basically it was a percussion band with an insignificant string accompaniment, for though the Fijians are great singers, their natural instrument is the drum and in their drumming I doubt they can be excelled by any other people.

The band started with a slow magnificent beat on the large drum. Then came a smaller drum in double time and then one smaller still with three beats to the deep single beat of the big drum. Soon a magnificent pattern of rhythm was being woven on the drums and when this had reached a peak it died away to the single beat.

Then the dancers came in. They were all young girls in their middle and late teens, plump and chocolate brown, their skin gleaming with perfumed coconut oil. They wore grass skirts, and leis made of dyed coconut fiber around their necks. They wore flowers twined into the fiber and had pendants of dyed fiber hanging from each lei.

The building was filled with the fragrance of jasmine. The dancers seated themselves before us and performed their dance with their hands, heads and shoulders. Each had made for herself a tiara of coconut sticks with the breast feathers of hens attached to the ends.

It is quite impossible for me to describe the grace and enchantment of this kind of dancing with the hands. Upper and lower arms, wrists, hands and fingers each performed the motions with a fluid movement that was the essence of grace. After awhile I could watch only the arms and hands and fingers whose movements were incredibly light and soft. Each dance told a story and while it was going on the girls chanted the tale which their hands were acting out. At the end of the *meke* I looked at the girl sitting opposite me and recognized the one who had been fishing and had thought to frighten me with the octopus. She was still in a teasing mood for she would turn to the girl next to her after giving me a bold look, say something, and then they would both fall to giggling.

When the *meke* was finished we were all served slices of bread which was very good. Then we were given bowls of *yangona*. And then the band started again, not with the haunting chants of Fiji now, but the songs of western ballrooms.

A tall and splendid Fijian came over to one of the women from the *Maroro* and tapped her on the foot. She looked frightened. "He just wants you to dance with him," I said. She got up to dance.

It was my turn next. Wallflowers are not permitted at Fiji dances. The fishing girl came over, put her lei around my neck and tapped me on the foot and I rose to dance with her. The dance was impossible. My own dancing had died off with the demise of the foxtrot though I once persuaded two English schoolteachers in Ireland to give me lessons in the twist. But that is another story.

The girl did not even know the foxtrot. She tried to move her feet in cadence with the music but we walked on each other's toes all the time. We danced about a foot apart from each other which isn't very comfortable and I attempted to hold her closer but she resisted this. So we stumbled about until the orchestra stopped when I returned her to her place and went to mine. The others of the party were asked to dance again and again by being tapped upon the foot. But I was ignored and wondered whether I had been guilty of some social error.

"No," said Stan when I asked him. "It is just that with your beard they think you are a missionary."

The others went on dancing and enjoying themselves for the rest of the evening but I sat glumly aside, suffering for the first time in my life from being bearded.

Chapter Twenty-one

THAKOMBAU Rex reigned as king of Fiji for seven troubled years. He was a man unique in world history, in that wishing to be a subject he was forced instead to become a monarch. His pleas for adoption by Great Britain of the Fiji Islands had been rejected. His Tongan enemies, once his friends, led by Ma'afu set up a Confederation of Northern and Eastern Fiji which included a great deal of the island of Vanua Levu. They were on the road to conquest, representing, as they insisted, Christianity. It was to counter this move that Thakombau, acting on the advice of white residents, set up his own government and made himself king of the remainder of the Fiji group though he claimed sovereignty over all.

The flag of the new kingdom—on a blue field a rising sun with a crown in the top corner—was raised; a meeting of native chiefs was held and the constitution of the monarchy (based on that of Hawaii) explained to them. Almost three hundred took an oath to uphold the king and the constitution and shortly afterwards Thakombau wished they hadn't.

He had hardly become king before the first and only missionary to be killed in Fiji was clubbed and eaten—the Reverend Baker already referred to. Responsibility was immediately placed at the door of Thakombau, though the murder had occurred among an inland tribe who were not really subject to him. A British ship arrived to avenge the deed but the captain was persuaded to leave the matter in the hands of Thakombau as sovereign. To do him justice, he tried his best to bring the murderers to court. But all expeditions, including one which Thakombau led himself, failed. Thakombau was shamed by the failure of his expedition in which he lost sixty men.

Thakombau's position as King of Fiji was made untenable by the same whites who had advised him to set up a monarchy. They were for the most part British subjects. They had no intention whatever of becoming subjects of Thakombau whom they called among themselves "the Cannibal King." They wanted him to be king over the Fijians and not over them, and they were warned by the British Consul of the serious consequences of submission to a foreign government.

These whites, then, would not pay any taxes. They were the richest people in the islands, they had benefited enormously out of the wealth of the islands, they proposed to continue to benefit in this way, but they would not contribute a penny to Thakombau's coffers.

The American Civil War which had disrupted the supply of cotton from the southern states to England brought a boom in cotton planting in Fiji. There had been sandalwood; there had been Bêche-de-Mer; now there was cotton and all without paying taxes of any kind. Fiji became a land of opportunity and scores of settlers poured in from Australia,—to develop the land to be sure—but they formed a powerful group which refused to be subject to the laws of Fiji. The boom in cotton brought a demand for labor and the Fijians were not interested in becoming plantation hands.

So the infamous traffic known as "blackbirding" came about. Laborers were brought into Fiji from the New Hebrides, from the Solomons, from the Gilbert, Ellice and Tokelau Islands. They were supposed to be working on contract with their passages paid home at the end of their term. Some of the planters had heart enough to observe these conditions. But the majority ignored them and the laborers were little more than slaves.

Some were sold into this kind of legal slavery by their own chiefs. Some were plainly kidnapped—enticed on board ships with offers of food and liquor, and tumbled below into the hold and the hatches battened down over them. Some were captured from their canoes when they innocently came along side a blackbirder's vessel to trade. A common practice was to drop pigs of iron from the ship's deck into the canoes, knocking holes in their bottoms. The natives, struggling in the water, were hauled on board and taken off to work on the plantations.

The blackbirders were a rascally but picturesque lot and the captain of a blackbirding schooner or brig received four dollars a head for every man he landed in the Fijis. Some, dressed in the dark clothing of missionaries, went ashore and preached moving sermons about the brotherhood of mankind and gave out a few little gifts. When they had collected a good crowd, their crew, armed with muskets and in ambush, rounded up the congregation and took them off to the plantations.

The islanders fought back and many blackbirders were greeted with flights of poisoned arrows as they dropped anchor in a bay that previously had welcomed ships. The British government stepped in to stop the trade, but it was difficult to prove slavery when a labor contract actually existed.

In one terrible case three natives kidnapped from a canoe in the New Hebrides were thrust into a hold containing seventy men of hostile tribes. A riot broke out in the hold which so frightened the ship's crew that the three men were taken out and shot and their bodies thrown overboard. In this case the captain was sentenced to life imprisonment.

In another instance, when a similar riot broke out in the hold of the brig *Carl* where there were eighty men, the crew fired muskets down the hatch to stop the fighting. When the hatches were opened the following morning, the hold resembled a slaughter house. Fifty men were dead either from bullets or spears made out of the splinters from bunks with which the frenzied islanders had fought each other. Twenty-five were horribly wounded and only five were able to climb out of the hatch unaided.

To remove all the evidence of this atrocity, dead and wounded were flung overboard to the sharks. But a white man aboard, who was a part owner of the vessel and incidentally a doctor, confessed the crime to the British Consul at Levuka when the ship called there. Having turned Queen's evidence, this man, Doctor Murray, was set free but the captain and one other were found guilty of murder and hanged.

Great Britain now put pressure on King Thakombau and his government to pass legislation to control the traffic in blackbirding. Thakombau did his best. But it was the whites who were engaged in blackbirding and they did not recognize his authority. With the aid of their consuls they evaded the regulations. Eventually the British government had to act itself in Fiji to stamp out blackbirding. The fact that Britain did have to act in Fiji pointed up the need for a real authority in the Fijis and opened the way for final acceptance by Great Britain of the Fiji Islands as a colony.

Before this acceptance came, however, a group of whites in Levuka circulated a petition for annexation by the United States. The petition read in part: "We the undersigned ... earnestly pray that you will at an early date announce to the world your resolve to extend the protection of your flag to these islands and waters permanently." The petition was addressed to the President of the United States, Rutherford B. Hayes, and seventy signatures were appended to it.

One suspects the subtle mind of Thakombau at work. He was still unlettered and could only with great difficulty sign his name. But fearsome as he was a warrior he was far more potent as an intriguer. He may well have sensed the rivalry between Britain and America and decided to make use of it to nudge Britain into accepting dominion over the Fijis.

He knew now beyond any shadow of a doubt that the Fijis must be protected by one white power or they would be utterly destroyed either by being swallowed by the Tongans or torn to pieces by the rivalries of the whites. A war with the Tongans loomed closer and closer and Thakombau knew that if it broke out, it would be the bloodiest war in which the islands had ever been plunged. He was a tyrant but he loved his people. He was the first Fijian chief ever to be able to visualize them as a whole, to be able to think of them as Fijians rather than as members of different tribes. He wanted to save Fiji and he put the whole resources of his mind to that end.

The petition to the United States President was presented to the United States Vice-Consul at Levuka, forwarded to the United States Consul-General in Australia where more signatures were added and eventually found its way to the State Department in Washington. The British reacted immediately. The Foreign Office in London pressed the Colonial Office to take action to protect the interests of British subjects resident in Fiji.

The Colonial Office was still unwilling to advise taking over the islands. Inquiries were made in Washington by the British who received America's assurance that the United States had no desire to annex the Fiji Islands. This permitted a breathing space.

Thakombau once again reformed his government, redrafted the Constitution, set up a House of Delegates to which representatives were elected and at the first meeting of this new House in which most of the delegates were Europeans, Thakombau said in his address, "Fiji is a dark land and we look to you (whites) for light as to law and civilization." They applauded and gave him no help.

They wanted the chiefs to rule the Fijians while they ruled

170

themselves and reaped the profits. There was in Fiji, then, a perfectly good government on paper but an utter lack of government in reality. The blackbirding trade was becoming an international disgrace and Thakombau was not above selling prisoners captured in little local wars to the blackbirders. It may be said in his defense that this was an improvement on the older tradition of clubbing and eating them, and furthermore he had a desperate need of money to run his government and the whites refused to contribute through taxes to his coffers.

A commission was sent from England to investigate the situation on the islands as a result of the stir about blackbirding. Thakombau was somewhat cold to the commissioners but in the end he announced that he was willing to cede the islands to Great Britain. He wrote a letter in which he stated that, "It is our mind to give government of our kingdom to the Lady Queen of Great Britain."

Invited to lunch on board HMS *Pearl* which had brought the commissioners, he proposed the Queen's health with these word, "Queen Victoria: We trust in her goodness; we give ourselves this day to her."

The commissioners' report, with Thakombau's renewed offer of cession, reached England when Disraeli had become Prime Minister. Disraeli believed in the expansion of the British Empire. Still England hesitated and another commissioner was sent to Fiji to examine the whole situation again. Whatever may be said of British colonialism in the nineteenth century, certainly the annexation of the Fiji Islands is a classic example of reluctant imperialism.

Sir Hercules Robinson was sent to Fiji on HMS *Pearl* which had the grace to salute Thakombau with twenty-one guns as King of Fiji. Sir Hercules, interviewing Thakombau, said that Her Majesty, Queen Victoria, was willing to accept sovereignty over Fiji but the terms previously outlined would hamper Her Majesty in the good government of the country.

There was about Thakombau a towering dignity—an absence of niggling which is the hallmark of a gentleman. The reply he made would have come well from the fairest knights of Europe in the days of chivalry, though delivered by a man who had eaten his fellows and assisted at the strangling of his own mother.

"The Queen is right; the conditions are not chieflike," Thakombau replied. "I was myself, from the first opposed to them but was overruled. If I give a chief a canoe and he knows that I expect something from him, I do not say 'I give you this canoe on condition of your only sailing it on certain days, or of your not letting such and such a man on it, or of your only using a particular kind of rope on it'; but I give him the canoe right out and trust to his generosity and good faith to make me the return he knows I expect. If I were to attach conditions, he would say, 'I do not care to be bothered with your canoe; keep it yourself.'

"Why should we have any anxiety about the future? What is the future? Britain. . . . If matters remain as they are Fiji will become like a piece of driftwood on the sea and be picked up by the first passerby. The whites who have come to Fiji are a bad lot. They are mere stalkers on the beach. . . . Of one thing I am assured, that if we do not cede Fiji, the white stalkers on the beach, the cormorants, will open their maws and swallow us. By annexation the two races, white and black, will be bound together and it will be impossible to sever them. The interlacing has come . . . law will bind us together and the stronger nation will lend stability to the weaker."

Two days later, after a discussion with his chiefs, Thakombau announced, "We give Fiji unreservedly to the Queen of Britain that she may rule us justly and affectionately, and that we may live in peace and prosperity."

A deed of cession was formally signed and the act was done. All that remained was the public announcement which took place at Nasova outside Levuka on the island of Ovalau on

October 10, 1874. Two hundred sailors and marines from British warships lined up by the flagstaff on which the colors of Thakombau, King of Fiji, were flown. The cession of the islands to Great Britain was announced to the islanders, Thakombau's flag run down and Britain's royal standard hoisted.

Thakombau had one more gesture to make after signing the deed of cession in public together with the other chiefs. Through his Chief of State, J. B. Thurston, he addressed the British commissioner Sir Hercules Robinson with these words.

"Before finally ceding his country to Her Majesty the Queen of Great Britain and Ireland, the king desires, through Your Excellency, to give Her Majesty the only thing he possesses that may interest her. The king gives Her Majesty his old and favorite war club, the former, and until lately, the only known law of Fiji. In abandoning club law and adopting the forms and principles of civilized society, he has laid aside his old weapon and covered it with emblems of peace.

"Many of his people, whole tribes, died and passed away under the old law; but hundreds of thousands will survive to enjoy the newer and better state of things. The king adds only a few words. With this emblem of the past, he sends his love to Her Majesty, saying he fully confides in her and her children who succeeding her shall become kings of Fiji, to exercise a watchful control over the welfare of his children and people who, having survived the barbaric law and age, are now submitting themselves under Her Majesty's rule to civilization."

Thakombau then handed the club which he had had decorated in silver with a design of ferns and doves to Sir Hercules Robinson. It had never left his hands before.

Chapter Twenty-two

W HEN Thakombau finally succeeded in abdicating as King of Fiji, he went with his two sons to visit New South Wales in Australia. There he contracted measles and on returning to Fiji, the three were convalescent but still infectious. Crowds assembled to welcome him home and shortly thereafter, there having been no quarantine precaution taken, the worst epidemic in the history of Fiji swept through the islands. So many died that in some villages the living were incapable of burying the dead. The death rate has never been ascertained but was estimated at a quarter of the population.

Medical facilities were utterly inadequate and the Fijians themselves had no concept of how to treat this strange illness. Raging with fever, the victims plunged into the rivers and sea to cool themselves with fatal effects. It was not long before they began to fear that this was a visitation on them from their gods for having thrown over their old religion and become subjects of the white men.

Some of the chiefs of the hill tribes—from the area that was known as the devil country because the people there had never become Christian nor given up cannibalism—had come to Suva at this time. They agreed to renounce heathenism and cannibalism and be subject to the government of the whites. When they returned to their own territory they carried measles with them and their people died in great numbers. They naturally took this to be a manifestation of anger on the part of their gods but some maintained that the disease was deliberately spread by the white man to wipe them out.

These "devil tribes" attacked villages belonging to Christian Fijians and killed and ate many of their inhabitants. Sir Arthur Gordon had been appointed Governor of Fiji. He had to act immediately and without calling for help from the small British forces on the islands, he raised an army of Fijians to seize the culprits. The Fiji chieftains responded enthusiastically to his request for men and the expedition against the offenders was a complete success. A number were seized, tried and executed for murder. That was the last great uprising in Fiji and it had been put down by Fijians though under the leadership of a white governor.

Thakombau now withdrew from public affairs except to lend his fullest support with complete loyalty to the new Governor. There were many around him, particularly disaffected whites, who tried to make him discontented so that he would use his influence to obstruct the new government. But he would not be drawn into these petty plots.

Sir Arthur Gordon was of the Scottish nobility and familiar in his own country with the clan system whereby members of a clan were loyal to their chief and ready to serve them. He saw in the tribes of Fiji a parallel to the Scottish clans and worked among the Fijians through their chiefs, never trying to break the people away from the leadership and allegiance to their own chieftains. A kind of inner government was established for the Fijians so that they would not be harmed in the conduct of their own affairs but would be permitted to live in their villages as they had done in the past.

Sir Arthur realized that if the Fijians were separated from their land they would quickly be destroyed. So an act was passed forbidding the sale by the Fijians of any of their lands to white settlers. The whites might rent land from the Fijians or buy certain lands called "crown lands" to which none of the tribes of Fiji laid any claim. But they could not, whatever price was offered, take away from the Fijians lands that belonged communally to a tribe.

A Land Claims Commission was set up to investigate the title to lands already sold to Europeans. The commission found some of the Europeans claiming vast acreages on the strength of a piece of paper with an undecipherable signature on it, quite often not that of the legal owner. Well over a thousand claims were investigated and of these less than half were found to be just.

In establishing a firm and fair government of the Fiji Islands, Gordon ran into considerable trouble from white settlers and somewhat surprisingly from the missionaries. The settlers expected that everything would go their way when the islands became a British protectorate. They were horrified when they discovered that the Fijians were to be protected and not exploited and tried to discredit Gordon, but without success.

The missionaries, in the last years of Thakombau's reign, had had great influence in the government. They were chagrined to find that their recommendations were not always followed and indeed that they were often crossed by the government. Sir Arthur Gordon had a great deal of admiration for the Wesleyan missionaries but in late years they had become overbearing and narrow. He discovered that money was being taken from the people by the missionaries with the assistance of Fijian magistrates and with threats of imprisonment if they didn't pay up. In effect a mission tax was being levied under the pretense that it was supported by the government.

Sir Arthur immediately forbade magistrates to support the missionaries in these collections and ordered any money so collected to be refunded. According to Sir Arthur the chief effort of the missionary after that "was to regain his lost ascendency or failing that to destroy what had superceded it, namely the colonial government. The head of the mission," he said, "had occupied in the past very much the position of the political bishops of the middle ages . . . accustomed to rule very autocratically in much outside the spiritual sphere."

The missionaries also objected to the government's recognition of the validity of marriages contracted in accordance with Fijian custom, and they were angry at the government which did not support their own objections to dancing. Sir Arthur wrote to the Wesleyan Mission in 1880 saying that the government would prohibit immoral or indecent dances but not harmless dancing in the daytime, wrestling or running or playing ball, to all of which the missionaries objected. He reprimanded them for puritanism and said that they were making it sinful for girls to wear flowers or make artificial flowers of feathers at which they were expert.

There still remained the problem of labor. The Fijians were not inclined to work for wages. They had no ambition to amass individual wealth and no conception of privately owned property. They were rather like the red Indian of the United States in that all they owned was owned by the tribe. They lived within the framework of the tribe, shared the tribe's tasks and wished no other kind of life. But the whites needed labor for their growing plantations.

Sugar was beginning to replace cotton and copra was booming and there was a need for workers. The blackbirders were now forbidden to operate by strong laws preventing the kidnapping of people for plantation work. In any case the South Sea area has no real labor surplus. And so the government imported laborers on contract from the teeming millions of India and a wholly foreign population was introduced into Fiji to supply the labor shortage—East Indians.

A total of some sixty-two thousand East Indians were brought from India between 1879 and 1916 when the system was abolished. They came on indentures by which they were to work five years in return for agreed wages and accommodations. The laborer could then work another five years for himself or for anyone he pleased, and after that he was entitled to free passage back to India for himself and his family. Only about a third of the Indians brought over returned to their homeland. The remainder settled in Fiji, bought crown lands and took to farming. They were hard workers and able to drive a sharp bargain. They differed in this respect from the Fijians. At the last census there were more East Indians in Fiji than Fijians and this imbalance, coupled with the fact that the two peoples are utterly strange to each other, constitutes one of the major problems for the future.

Fijian and Indian live side by side but with hardly any intermingling for a variety of reasons. First, they do not speak the same language. To be sure in the towns of Fiji, such as Suva and Lautoka, Indians and Fijians can speak English. But English is a foreign tongue for both of them and they cling to their own languages. The Fijian does not learn Hindustani. The Indian does not learn Fijian.

Education could dissolve this barrier but there is no real compulsory education of children in Fiji. The law requires Fijian children to go to school between the ages of six and fourteen if there is a school within three miles of the child's home. Among Fijians the literacy rate is high and ninety-two percent of Fijian children can read and write. There is no compulsory education of Indian children and although schools are available for them the literacy rate among Indians, particularly girls, is low.

One of the problems of schooling is the language difficulty. Indian children have to be taught in Indian schools where the teachers can speak Hindustani. Fijians are taught in Fijian schools where the teachers speak Fijian. A segregation of the two races cannot be avoided, even in their schooling.

Again Indian and Fijian are separated by religion. The Fijian is a Christian, the Indian, Hindu. They cannot, then, even worship together. Added to this, the Fijian is the aboriginal inhabitant of the island, owns the greater part of the land and the British government, bent upon protecting him, has

178

made it impossible for him to sell his land. The Indian is a farmer but one who cannot get title to the land he farms in many cases. He may buy Crown lands but they are not always the best farming land. He may rent Fijian land, but the Indian finds sugar his best crop and the good sugar lands are already largely owned by big sugar companies.

These are but the generalities of a complex problem. Between Indian and Fijian at the present time there is coexistence. What is needed and is inevitable, is integration and a common purpose—the prosperity of the peoples and the islands of Fiji in which the Indians have now lived for three or four generations while remaining Indians.

Chapter Twenty-three

THAKOMBAU died in great dignity and honor in 1883. A British warship saluted his passing with mourning guns and the whole of the Fijis observed his funeral with great solemnity. His life had been almost beyond the extravagances of fiction. In his youth he was the most fearsome of the savages, the leader of the pagan forces, the man who insisted on the strangling of five women to adorn his father's funeral.

In his manhood he recognized the inevitable advance of civilization, the terrible changes that lay ahead for his people, and he led them as safely as he might and with great dignity into the white man's world. He was not deceived by civilization. He saw its pettinesses as well as its virtues. He could distinguish between the self-seeking whites who looked only for their own gain and the others, some of them the early missionaries, who genuinely sought the improvement of the lot of his people.

No man, when he was a pagan, was a greater pagan than Thakombau. No man, when he was a Christian, was a greater Christian. When he renounced his sovereignty and handed over the islands he loved to the care of the British Crown, in the person of Sir Arthur Gordon, he insisted on a public ceremony of submission to the British government. It was a touching ceremony in the Fijian tradition. He himself publicly laid an immense root of *yangona* at Sir Arthur's feet and broke off a portion and placed it in Sir Arthur's hand—the traditional Fijian act of submission and homage. Only a great man would voluntarily undergo such a public submission. It implied a complete surrender by Thakombau and a complete trust in the British Crown.

Colonialism is unfashionable these days. It should be stated that the British rule of Fiji has always been directed at protecting the Fijians from the exploitation of the whites. In that it has succeeded and to this day the Fijis are among the few islands in the South Seas where the people are permitted to continue with the communal tribal life they developed through the centuries. Their customs are respected and honored and the whites seek to earn for themselves the respect of the Fijians who, even in their darkest days, put a high value on good manners.

Unfortunately protection involves protection from change and in Fiji, because of the importation of the East Indian workers, the Fijian falls behind in the economic struggle of the twentieth century. Living in the country and on the small islands under his chiefs, working communally in his village without thought of private wealth, he cannot compete with the industrious Indian, who has become economically and politically more powerful.

Some of the Fijians want to put an end to the communal living. They want to be able to get out and compete with the East Indian but these are the minority though, if a stranger may venture an opinion, they may also represent the future. The Indians for their part, who have labored now for several generations in Fiji, would like to see the lands of Fiji made available to them for purchase. That would mean the end of the old Fijian tribal system and perhaps the end of many Fijian customs which hold the people together in pride of race.

The problem will not be solved without much suffering and perhaps a loss of values of which the world, as much as Fiji, stands in need—such values as loyalty to one's people, communal service on behalf of one's people and what Thomas

Jefferson called the pursuit of happiness—happiness expressed not in worldly goods but in an easy and innocent and rewarding method of living.

When I last arrived in Fiji it was at the International Airport at Nandi. The airport is one hundred and forty miles by a winding road from Suva and you may get to the capital either by a Fiji Airways plane or by a chartered taxi which are all run by Indians. I decided to take a taxi and share it with such others as were also making the journey.

One of my fellow passengers was a tall, well-made Fijian. To while away the journey we fell to talking. He was reluctant to discuss his affairs but finding that I was a writer confessed that he himself was a politician who had, incidentally, previously been a boxer. His name he said was Apimeleki Ramatau Kataka. He had been, he told me, in jail as a result of his political activities but I think the reason he was jailed was for disturbing the peace though the charge against him was dismissed.

He told me of his ambitions for Fiji. He said he wanted to see the authority of the chiefs abolished, and the people now living communally under the chiefs, free to go about their own enterprises and sell their land if they wished. If this was not done, he felt, the Fijian people would be pushed to the wall by their Indian rivals and he was sure that his people, once they made the break from tribal existence could compete successfully with the Indians. He wanted, I think, to see an end to the sort of inner government of the Fijians which was set up to protect them and give them, through their chiefs, a say in the general government of the island so that their ways were not destroyed. He told me that people called him a Communist but he denied that he was one. He then asked me for my advice.

I told him I was a stranger to Fiji and it would be impertinent of me to offer advice. But I asked him to consider what was his aim.

"The welfare of my people," he replied.

"You must consider," I said, "whether their welfare and happiness will be increased if they all own automobiles, have bank balances and can buy television or radio sets. You must consider whether happiness consists in goods or in a way of life that does not necessarily lead to the accumulation of goods."

"But we must be free," he replied. "We must not be subject to the authority of a chief who can take the profits of men's work and keep them for himself."

With that I had to agree though I said I did not know that this was the case. I mention the man because he is, whether a villain or a hero, one leader of the new thought among Fijians—a kind of discontent (not I think very widespread) with the old living and a fear that, if continued, it will bring the Fijian into an economic and perhaps political inferiority to the Indian. When we reached Suva, my Fijian politician became pure Fijian.

"You have somewhere to stay?" he asked.

"No, I will find a hotel," I replied.

"They are very crowded at this time of the year, sir. If you are unable to find a hotel I would be honored if you would come and stay in my home."

Although he had other business of his own, he remained with me to his own inconvenience until he was sure that I would have a roof over my head that night.

Around the marketplace in Suva at nighttime you may find a group of Fijians seated on the pavement with a bowl of *yangona*. I passed such a group just before leaving Fiji and on their invitation sat on the pavement with them. They made a little living serving *yangona* at a penny or two a drink. They spoke English and I asked them how they had come to leave their own villages and islands. In some cases they had been attracted to the city by one opportunity or another— a friend working in Suva, desire to see the town and share in its seemingly exciting life, and so on. When I left, one of these women looked at me and said earnestly, "Promise me that things are going to be better for us."

"I hope they are going to be better for you," I said.

"No. No." she said. "Do not say you *hope* they will be better, say you *know* they will be better." There were, to my surprise, tears on her cheeks.

"Things will be better for you," I said.

I trust with all my heart that I did not lie, but the transition from the communal life of the village to the individual life of private money and private property is going to be hard indeed on many Fijians. Still, they are a brave and generous people and will make the change eventually without, I trust, losing their heritage.

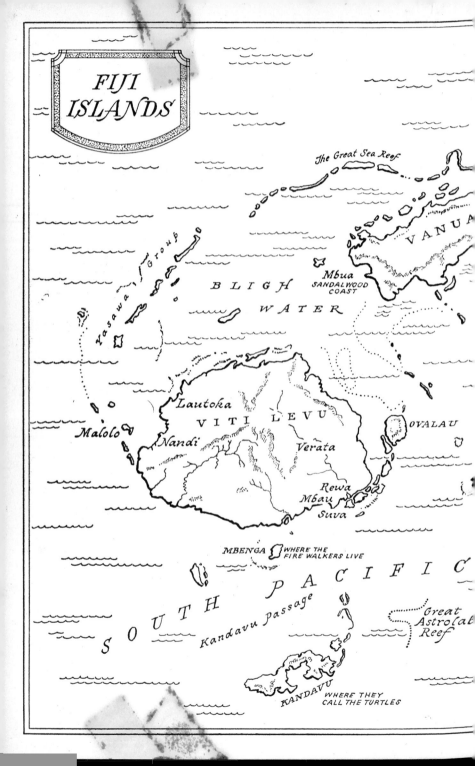